NOSHING IS SACRED

NOSHING IS SACRED

Israel Shenker

The Bobbs-Merrill Company, Inc.
Indianapolis·New York

Copyright © 1979 by Israel Shenker
Introduction copyright © 1979 by Russell Baker
All rights reserved, including the right of reproduction
in whole or in part in any form
Published by The Bobbs-Merrill Company, Inc.
Indianapolis   New York

Designed by Rita Muncie
Manufactured in the United States of America

First printing

Library of Congress Cataloging in Publication Data

Shenker, Israel.
  Noshing is sacred.

  1. Cookery, Jewish—Addresses, essays, lectures.
2. Jews in the United States—Social life and
customs.   I. Title.
TX724.S5   641   79–11872
ISBN 0-672-52600-X

For Mona Sagman, my mother-in-law,
renowned beyond all borders for the splendor of
her soup;
remarkable beyond the common measure
for her spirit, wit and plain speaking.

My thanks go to editors at *The New York Times* for valor in page-to-page combat as many of the words printed in this book battled past them en route to newspaper mortality. My appreciation goes to S. J. Perelman for suggesting the title.

Contents

Introduction

MY FATHER'S PEOPLE were country folk who shared the rustic preoccupation with innards. Gastric distress was as much a part of their daily routine as stoking the wood stove and carrying water from the spring. In fact, I was far gone in the decay of an urban adolescence before I discovered that indigestion and heartburn—or "gas," as all digestive rebellions were called around our house—were not part of humanity's birthright.

At our house the favored specific for this ailment was a powder called Bisodol. Some of my earliest memories are of desperate adults prowling the halls in the predawn darkness, crying, "Where's the Bisodol?" At certain feasts—Thanksgiving, Christmas, funerals, visits by relatives who had moved up in the world and rated a three-pie salute to conclude the meal—the Bisodol was kept in a canister over the kitchen sink to be more readily available in emergencies.

The food that produced this antacid tycoon's dream of Paradise was different in content from what Israel Shenker discusses in the following pages, but not in weight. Unrestrained by Talmudic injunction, we partook insensately of the porker. We mixed dairy, flesh and shellfish with an abandon that would have appalled all dietary science, as well as any sensible stalwart of Jewry, had there been any in the vicinity to witness the debauch.

Slices of cured ham were pan-fried in the morning, along with eggs and potato pancakes or, sometimes, sausage cakes that had been preserved in grease in sealed Mason jars. Fried oysters for breakfast was not unknown. School lunch at its most substantial was a slice of fried "country ham" congealed between slices of homemade bread, the whole thing cooled, to set the grease, by four hours of storage in a metal lunch box.

Steak, when available at all, was fried in a skillet until it reached the consistency of leather. Pole beans and new potatoes came to the table floating in tureens of ham liquor. For dessert we gorged on fruit pies, cakes so damp and rich it took strong men to carry them to the table, pickled watermelon rind, sweet potatoes mashed to a purée with big dollops of vanilla and sugar, and similar delicacies which I forbear to describe out of respect for the gentler reader.

Later I discovered that dining on this scale was not the universal habit, even in those parts of the world fortunate enough to be able to afford it, and, indeed, that many cultures regarded it as barbaric. The French, I believe, are responsible for this. If I correctly understand the philosophy of French cuisine, it holds any meal that produces acute pain throughout the upper torso to be an offense against Western civilization.

I have never been at ease with this theory. Many nights when I wake at 3 A.M. with sharp pain under the breastbone, I am comforted by thinking back upon the heavy tonnage taken aboard at the dinner hour and reflecting that this is not the dreadful coronary seizure the world keeps promising me, but only the glorious old "gas" so vital to the survival of my ancestors.

Jewish cuisine differs from that of my fathers in both philosophy and content, but in its preoccupation with food as a gesture of love, the two have much in common. If the price we pay for that gesture be a little pain in the night, a little agony on the bathroom scales, a prowl down dark corridors groping for the Bisodol—well, who said love was all roses without a thorn?

Russell Baker
April, 1979

Preface

LET THE BUYER BEWARE! This is not a cookbook. Heaven preserve the reader from any recipe I could invent. All of my experience in the kitchen has taught me that survival depends on letting someone else do the cooking.

This book does hint delicately about how Jewish food is approached and consumed—as though there were not a moment to spare in the struggle between raging appetite and splendid overindulgence.

There is a smattering of arcane knowledge gleaned from experts whose appetites are rarely slaked, an abundance of blessings (one chapter tells which are appropriate), and a leaven of plagues (warnings of heartburn are sprinkled liberally). There are chapters about food to grow fat on, food to wax nostalgic about, food that's kosher and more that's not, and testimony on how to keep body and soul together—or apart. There are visits to shrines—a matzoh factory, a *knish* factory, a food show, and a hotel where weeks are counted in smoked salmon. Illustrious hungry men—Isaac Bashevis Singer, S. J. Perelman—parade their appetites here.

Most of this material has appeared, in one form or another, in *The New York Times*, where I was a reporter from 1968 to 1979.

It would be a gross miscarriage of intention if any of this made you wiser. If it makes you hungrier, bravo!

NOSHING IS SACRED

American Jewish Cooking

A FRENCHMAN says "Taste!" but a Jewish cook says "Eat!" In France a gourmet appreciates the artistry of the chef and develops a discriminating and educated palate. Palate shmalate! In the world of Jewish food, people who have wasted their education on a palate are known not as gourmets but as finicky eaters. The way to approach a Jewish meal is not delicately, but on the run. An appropriate thing to say, though one hardly has time to say it, is "I'm fainting with hunger."

From his earliest a Jewish child would hear his mother's entreaty: *"Ess!"* (Eat!) A child had to be fattened to meet life's trials. "Fix yourself!" was the ritual phrase, meaning "Eat and put on weight." No child was sent to bed without supper; for a Jewish child, *not* eating was a form of passive resistance. Very effective!

In English translation, a popular Yiddish song goes:

> *Friday, Saturday, Sunday,*
> *As each guest arrives,*

> *Every mother sits and watches*
> *How her baby thrives.*
> *"Eat and eat and eat and stuff,*
> *And eat, my lovely son,*
> *Eat and eat and eat and stuff,*
> *And soon you'll weigh a ton."*

Fannie Scharfstein, who lives on the Lower East Side of New York City, said: "I used to have quarrels with my husband, and then I would serve him and leave the room; I would never dream of not feeding him."

Nostalgia is the essential ingredient. The son remembers that for his mother a cold meal was next to godlessness and that he should "Eat first and talk later." If anything was left on the plate, it was a sign he did not love his mother.

American Jewish nostalgia is the product of scores of regional sources abroad, just as the cooking is strongly influenced by non-Jewish food. Eggplant specialties, for example, came from the Balkans, goulash from Hungary, dumplings from Czechoslovakia, shtrudel from the Austro-Hungarian Empire. Even though the modern Jewish wife pays lip service to the virtues of slimness, she has no stomach for it. If the result of overeating is overweight, is that a sin? Is it not written in the Talmud that "Man will be called to account in the hereafter for each enjoyment he declined on earth without sufficient cause"?

For those who respect tradition, Jewish mothers rule the kitchen unchallenged, and virtually all of them are said to have been great cooks. Author Isaac Bashevis Singer has an explanation for this: "Their sons were big liars."

In the villages and ghettos of Eastern Europe, many Jews ate a substantial meal only on the Sabbath eve, surviving the rest of the week on bread, potatoes, and—if they were fortunate—herring.

The first Jewish settlers—twenty-three of them—came to America in 1654. Since then about three million have immigrated, and the Jewish population is now about six million. Up to the 1880s, most Jewish immigrants came from Germany, and from then until 1914 about two million additional Jews fleeing persecution and poverty arrived from Russia, Poland, Austria-Hungary and Rumania. They usually came without money, settled in the humblest neighborhoods, and built up their own schools, synagogues, newspapers, trades, shops, home cooking and desperate optimism—"He that gave us teeth will give us bread." On the Lower East Side, streets were jammed with pushcarts, and the air throbbed with the redolence of fresh food and the cries of vendors. It was hard to starve and difficult to prosper.

In America as in Europe, observant Jews sought their guidelines in the Old Testament and in the commentaries of rabbis who had built an elaborate structure of regulations indicating which foods and cooking methods are kosher (conforming to Jewish dietary laws) and which are *trayf* (not kosher). "Whatsoever parteth the hoof, and is cloven-footed, *and* cheweth the cud, among the beasts, that shall ye eat" (Leviticus 11:3). Creeping animals are forbidden as food, and so are fish without fins and scales. Even the slaughtering of animals is circumscribed with religious laws.

In three places the Old Testament prohibits seething a kid in its mother's milk. This has evolved into the prohibition of meat (*flayshik*) and dairy (*milchik*) food at the same meal; dishes used for one may never be used for the other, or even washed together. A third category of food (in addition to meat and dairy) is called *pareve*. This consists of fish, vegetables, fruit, eggs and cereal. Because it is considered neither *flayshik* nor *milchik*, *pareve* may be eaten with either.

Today the laws are honored in the breach as well as by the observant. Many Jews dismiss the regulations as obsolete, academic, and certainly inconvenient. Others practice selective observance: they eat no pork, but love lobster; or they shun shellfish and dote on bacon.

Many of the specialties—kosher or *trayf*—are now widely popular. What began as *gehakte leber*, a proletarian version of *pâté de foie gras*, is dignified these days as chopped liver. *Praakes* and *bolishkes* are honored as stuffed cabbage. *Kishke* has been anglicized into stuffed *derma*, though it is still the same long piece of filled beef casing that humorist Sam Levenson called "fire hose."

Cholent has not yet made the English grade, but it deserves to graduate. Since lighting a fire is prohibited on the Sabbath, this alloy of meat and other ingredients such as onions, beans, potatoes and barley was put into the oven on Friday afternoon and taken out the next day. It served as the Sabbath lunch.

Though it may be the stuffing that dreams are made on (one Hungarian rabbi said it cured insomnia), *cholent* is a linguist's nightmare. One derivation traces it to the past participle of a Latin verb meaning "to warm up," another to the French *chaud lent* (hot slow), and a third to the German *shul ende* (synagogue services are over).

Pot roast is another favorite, also known as *gedempte flaysh; essig flaysh* is a sweet-and-sour version. *Flanken* is flank steak. *Gefilte helzel* (stuffed chicken neck) may feature ingredients such as breadcrumbs, flour, onions and fat. *Pirogen* are hardly distinguishable from *piroshki* (their Russian and Polish forebears)—chopped, cooked meat mixed with onion, rolled in dough and baked. Served *with* soup, not in soup.

In years past, Jewish cooks learned their art from mothers, grandmothers or aunts and never wrote down recipes or measured ingredients. Mona Sagman remembers how it was when she sought instruction from her aunt Eda. " 'How do you make *tayglach* [a honeyed confection]?' I'd ask her, and she'd say in Yiddish, 'You take flour.' You'd say to her 'How much flour?' and she'd look at you as if you were mad and say, 'As much as you'll want *tayglach*.' Well, you accepted that, and you had some kind of vision in your mind what size bowl you would fill with flour, and then she'd say, 'You put in eggs,' and you'd say, 'How many eggs?' And again you'd get the look, and she'd say, 'As much as you'll have flour.' "

Fannie Cohen of New York City remembers learning how to make *lokshen* (noodles), and saying to her mother, "My hand is smaller than yours. What should I do?" Her mother said, "Take another handful."

"My mother makes a marvelous *veinek kugel* [a rich fruit pudding made with shtrudel dough]," said Anita Field, a Philadelphia housewife. "One day I decided to watch her making it and write down the recipe. She took a handful of flour, and I said, 'Stop!' and ran and got a cup and held it under her hand, so I'd know how much she put in. I measured everything in the same way, and I wrote it all down. When the dough was finished, she said, '*Oi vay!* It doesn't look right,' and began throwing things in left and right so fast that I couldn't measure a thing. I still don't know how to make the *kugel.* "

In Jewish cooking, that's the way the *kugel* crumbles, but even a crumbled *kugel* is no tragedy. The delicacy (usually made with noodles or potatoes—plus ingredients such as eggs, sugar, raisins and cinnamon) is known as the perfect food, because if it sticks together, you have a marvelous dish; and if it doesn't stick together, you have marvelous ingredients. Heinrich Heine, the German Jewish poet, called it "this holy national dish"; and Sholom Aleichem (who liked to think in terms of good, better, delicious) wrote: "Fat, fatter, *kugel.*"

Though Leo Rosten, author of *Joys of Yiddish,* maintains that Yiddish is a language without puns, his theory does not account for the joys of *tsimmes.* Off the table the word means "fuss," as in "Don't make such a *tsimmes.*" On the table it is a succulent dish, even a meal by itself, made from stewed vegetables, with or without fruit and beef. Sholom Aleichem writes about a marriage-maker who is treated so well at the prospective bride's home that "they serve me the best portions of meat and feed me *tsimmes* even on weekdays."

Any day of the week may be rich in *shmaltz*—rendered animal fat, usually from a chicken. "If you cut down on *shmaltz,* it's not Jewish cooking—it's American cooking," says Betty Solondz, a Long Island housewife. But others make such a *tsimmes* about cholesterol that they substitute margarine, shortening or vegetable oil. The word *shmaltz,* however, is still useful, having oozed from Jewish kitchens into the English language to designate anything overly sentimental.

Shmaltz even dignifies herring, which is traditionally a proletarian special. There are also other ways to dignify fish; e.g., by serving it as chopped herring—raw salt herring chopped together with an apple, onion, bread and vinegar. Golda Meir, who had all kinds of cabinets in her Israeli kitchen, told the story of a stingy father and generous mother. The mother insisted that her husband regularly bring guests from the synagogue for Friday night dinner, and she would begin by serving them pickled herring. "All right," the husband said, "you have to feed them; but do you have to build up their appetites?"

But who could live without fish? Sholom Aleichem

wrote that housewives would never dream of going home without fish for the Sabbath. "That's worse than dying, for if she had died it would be over and done with," he explained. "But if she comes home without fish for the Sabbath, then she has to face her husband's anger. And that's worse than death."

In America the quintessential specialty is *gefilte* (stuffed) fish—usually based on carp, but everyone to his own recipe. The classic specialty is made from fish scraped from skin and bones, chopped together with onions, eggs and breadcrumbs, then boiled or baked and served cold. In America it is usually made into round or oval shapes, and in any country at all the thing to eat with *gefilte* fish is horseradish dyed red with beet juice.

To soothe the fevered brow which follows, soup has traditionally been the thing. Chicken soup was considered the miracle of folk medicine and became known as Jewish penicillin. Author Charles Angoff recalls that his great-grandmother used to say: "If chicken soup and sleep can't cure you, nothing will."

The soup is often served with *lukshen* (noodles), graphic testimony to the wisdom that "Love is grand, but love with *lukshen* is even better." *Knaydlach* (matzoh balls), made with matzoh meal, eggs and fat, are equally welcome in chicken soup. Some enthusiasts like them light, and others feel shortweighted by *knaydlach* that rise to the surface.

Many prefer *kreplach* in the soup, though. *Kreplach*—boiled or fried, stuffed with meat or cheese—may also be served without soup. Traditionally these Jewish relatives of ravioli and won ton are eaten three times a year: on Yom Kippur, when you beat your breast; on Hoshana Raba, when you beat the ground with willow branches; and during Purim, when you beat the floor with your feet at mention of the name Haman. You eat *kreplach* a fourth time during the year, so the story goes, when you beat your wife to get her to make them again.

Mushroom-barley soup stands close to chicken soup on the scale of popularity, and not far behind is borsht—beet soup—familiar in the expression "You don't know from borsht." Split pea soup has the aura of Dutch *erwtensoep,* and vegetable soup is minestrone with a Yiddish accent.

Accentuating the negative is the pride of Jewish dairy restaurants. Their menus abound in meat-sounding dishes that have no meat. The chopped liver may be based on sardines; finely ground vegetables constitute the protose steak and the vegetable cutlet.

"When I was twenty, I became a vegetarian one morning," said Isaac Bashevis Singer, "and in the evening I had a terrible desire for a frankfurter." He finally summoned the strength to become a vegetarian and to write stories in which butchers have nightmares about the slaughterhouse. He also found a restaurant which, as he noted, "makes such a good chopped liver you can't tell it from chopped liver."

"The only thing that tempts me now is *flanken,*" he said.

Mr. Singer is also enthusiastic about blintzes, and indeed who is not? Blintzes are golden pancakes (not quite so delicate as crêpes) rolled up with cottage cheese or fruit or chopped nuts or even poppy seeds inside, fried or baked, and served with sour cream and sometimes with fruit preserves as well.

Everything that's good is better with sour cream. This wholesome exaggeration holds strictly true for raw vegetables, fruits, potatoes, borsht, and herring, not to mention beef Stroganoff.

Some people will put sour cream even on *knishes* (the *k* is sounded, with or without sour cream), which are croquettes usually stuffed with potatoes, *kasha* (buckwheat groats), or meat. They are fried or baked and served hot.

The first time opera singer Jan Peerce entertained Arturo Toscanini at home, Jan's wife Alice conquered her nervousness and began the meal with *gefilte* fish and liver *knishes*. The Peerces had been warned that the maestro ate very little. "All of a sudden he was eating with both hands," Mrs. Peerce recalled. "One *gefilte* fish ball after another, one *knish,* another *knish.*" "Maestro, how can you eat so much Jewish food?" asked his host. "Jewish!" exclaimed Toscanini. "It's so good it *has* to be Italian."

Bella Krenzel, a Philadelphia housewife who was born in the Ukraine, remembers that her husband kept discovering different varieties of *knishes* made by other women: "He used to say the grocery lady made cabbage *knishes,* or *knishes* from beans. Who'd ever heard of such things! But I was jealous—so I made them. And when I made them, his favorite expression was 'Next year you'll make them again.' He meant he didn't really like them. He was a fussy eater, and I said to him, 'No wonder your sister was ready to pay me to marry you and take you away from her house.'"

Only the rare Jewish husband gives his wife her due. More common is an offhand appraisal—"*Men ken dus essen.*" (It's edible.) Reproached for not complimenting his wife on her cooking, the husband replies: "*Es darf ziyn gut!*" (It's *supposed* to be good!) The same husband who pretends to be indifferent will scrape his plate clean, discover an unused fork or spoon, and hold it aloft, saying, "This must be for something!"

If his enthusiasm is moderate, it is hardly her fault. The Jewish wife is no believer in modesty. She exclaims over her own *kreplach,* "They'll melt in your mouth." "This is delicious," she says as she serves her homemade borsht.

She is less enthusiastic about other women's cooking, and at restaurants she can be downright grudging. Tasting the soup, she may say, "They forgot to take out the fat," or, with equal conviction: "They took out all the fat. Do they call that soup?"

And what do they call a bagel? They call a doughnut-shaped roll a bagel—when made with a yeast dough first boiled in water, then baked in the oven until brown and very hard. No sugar, please—it's a bagel, not a doughnut. One theory is that bagels represent the mystery of life, since there's no easy way to get at them without breaking teeth.

A penumbra of pseudo-scholarship surrounds the bagel. One school maintains that centuries ago the Viennese were so grateful to their liberator, King Sobieski, that they clung to his horse's stirrup (*Bügel*, in German). A rival school maintains they were named not for *Bügel* but for Count Baigel, of saintly—if faint—memory, who stacked them on his billiard cue so that he could munch while he played.

There are even more variations than theories: egg bagels, onion bagels, garlic bagels, poppy seed bagels, cinnamon bagels, pumpernickel bagels, even green bagels on St. Patrick's Day.

Much less roundabout are the staple Jewish breads—especially rye and pumpernickel. The *challah*—made from white flour and egg and glazed with egg yolk—is the queen of braids.

Lekach (honey cake) and sponge are the cake staples. Sponge cake may be the only item in Jewish cuisine about which there is something like unanimity: it should be light, and the more eggs the better. Shtrudel is even higher in nostalgia content; thus, only grandmothers can make shtrudel, never mothers. The dough is rolled extremely thin. Inside are ingredients such as apples, cottage cheese, jam, cherries, raisins and nuts. Cheesecake is the favorite of

Jews emancipated, Jews traditional, and Jews whose grandmothers are too busy to make shtrudel.

With Jewish cooking, it's hard to know where cuisine leaves off and ritual starts; religious and holiday observances vary not only in prayer but also in food. From the commandment to honor God on the Sabbath there grew up the practice of eating a special meal on Friday night, when the Sabbath begins. The dinner usually starts with *gefilte* fish or chopped liver, moves on to chicken soup with trimmings, then chicken boiled or roasted—with *kugel.* Cake and lemon tea or coffee follow.

The *Pesach* (Passover) holiday commemorates the exodus from Egypt, when Moses led his people out of bondage. Honoring the Biblical account of the Jews' hurried flight with bread which had no time to leaven, observant Jews will eat only unleavened bread (matzoh) during the holiday. The first two nights are marked by special prayers and dinners including prescribed foods—such as bitter herbs recalling the bitterness of Egyptian slavery.

In America, Passover preparations in many homes have been reduced to one: purchasing matzoh. This unleavened bread is good with butter and salt, or fried with eggs to make matzoh *brei.*

On *Rosh haShanah* it is traditional to eat something sweet, such as apple slices dipped in honey, and to say the prayer: "May it be Thy will that this year shall be happy and sweet for us."

Yom Kippur is a solemn fast day, traditionally brought to a close with a meal of herring, boiled potatoes and sour cream, cakes and tea. The *challah* on this occasion has a dough ladder—strips across a long loaf—to help prayers rise to heaven.

Purim (Feast of Esther) is the time to eat *hamantashen,* tricornered cakes filled with plum or apricot jam, poppy seeds, or raisins—all in memory of the Biblical account of the villainy of Haman.

Hannukah (Festival of Lights) is the time for *latkes* (potato pancakes). One theory is that *latkes* are popular during *Hannukah* because they are easy to eat while playing cards.

Shavuot is a harvest festival, an occasion for eating cheese and milk products.

During *Sukkot* (Feast of the Tabernacles) religious Jews eat meals in a *sukkah*—a rudimentary outdoor shelter whose walls and ceiling are decorated with vegetables and fruit.

All year round the supreme indoor shelters are the Jewish delicatessens. Originally most were kosher; many are now "kosher style"—which means that they stock Jewish specialties, kosher or not. Many of the delicatessens have restaurant sections, and in exceptionally fancy establishments there are even tablecloths. Nostalgia sweeps through delicatessens like an avenging angel, refusing to forgive the counterman who butters bread for a corned beef sandwich (mixing meat and dairy!) or puts corned beef on white instead of rye (it spoils the taste).

Corned beef and pastrami—hot and sliced—are basic to the delicatessen's sandwich counter, and to "delicatessen" used as a noun to cover a multitude of other skins as well: salami, rolled beef, tongue, porkless frankfurters including the plump ones known as "specials," roast beef and turkey. One eats delicatessen in a delicatessen (just as one eats dairy in a dairy restaurant) or takes delicatessen home to eat it there, with coleslaw, potato salad, pickles, celery tonic or cream soda. In either place, there is nothing to surpass the delights of the delicatessen bagel spread with cream cheese and lox (smoked salmon) or Nova Scotia (lox with almost no salt).

Since Jewish housewives are stuck with the notion that only a home-cooked meal can satisfy the soul, they are less enthusiastic about delicatessen than their husbands. Many a housewife suspects that the family car is programmed to detour via the delicatessen to allow the husband a *nosh*. A *nosh* is more than a sample, less than a banquet. A *nosher* is a man training to become a *fresser*. A *fresser* is just a guy with a feed bag on who can't say when.

Shrines to *nosher* and *fresser* have blossomed. Detroit (birthplace of the detouring car) has about seventy delicatessens, including one whose owner calls his place "a corned beef happening." Atlanta has Happy Herman's and Sal's Ess'n Fress. Philadelphia boasts many delis, including one whose owner, Stanley Greenberg, complains: "I'd have to be a brain surgeon to cut a piece of corned beef the way some of my Jewish customers want it."

Before inflation was in flower, delicatessen owners used to offer pickles at "a nickel a *shtikel*" (piece). During World War II they advised: "Send a salami to your boy in the army."

Jewish delicatessens and restaurants are the only ones where you can get indigestion before your order arrives—from the sour pickles and the impatient waiters, high priests of chutzpah.

The waiter asks a customer if she wants *kasha varnitchkes* (buckwheat groats with twists of pasta). She says her doctor won't allow them. "You look healthy to me," says the waiter. "Change doctors."

A waiter at the Parkway East decides one customer is not doing justice to the food on his plate. He leans across the table, loosens the customer's tie, and opens the top button of the shirt. Then he takes up some food in a spoon and coaxes: "*Nem a layful.*" (Take a spoonful.)

Customers occasionally fight back. "This fish has gone bad," complains a customer in an ancient delicatessen story, "and why is the portion so small?"

Such worries never assail guests at bar mitzvahs or weddings. The caterer's slogan is: More is better, and less is a bad advertisement. This means acres of appetizers to stuff on, followed by an enormous meal. Legion are the legends of the banquet centerpiece—a statue of the bar mitzvah boy molded in chopped liver.

This is generations removed from the pioneer days of Jewish American cooking on the Lower East Side. Today the pushcarts have almost all disappeared, but not the heartburn of nostalgia. For those who cherish the good old ways, memory's delights are sold bottled, canned, frozen or fresh—commercial borsht, *gefilte* fish, corned beef, pastrami, rye bread and bagels. There is not yet a prayer to say over a thawing bagel, but somebody is surely working on it.

Kosher Gourmet

FOR THREE DAYS and nights, Rabbi Osher Shoretz patrolled the kitchens of the Waldorf-Astoria to make sure that the first ever gourmet kosher meal there really would be kosher. Sponsored by the Confrérie de la Chaîne des Rôtisseurs, the banquet would provide funds to help send an American team to Jerusalem to participate in the first International Conference and Exhibition on Jewish Culinary Art. Five kosher caterers provided the meat free, one sent in kosher pots and pans, and all signed up for a table apiece—$100 a stomach, ten stomachs per table.

Osher of the Waldorf, delegated by caterers Kotimsky & Tuchman, knew the hotel backwards and forwards, and also the dietary laws in both directions. For thirteen years he had served with Patrician caterers, and when K&T bought Patrician they acquired Rabbi Shoretz. "They got a bargain," is the way he put it.

Nothing escaped him. "I know all the movements of these people," he said. "They couldn't fool me a bit. Everything is under control. Take a look at the dishes. So clean even you can't see one Pesach."

When he heard that the gourmet kosher meal would be served with nonkosher wines, and that this might be publicized, Rabbi Shoretz announced he would stop the meal. Then he called Sidney Kotimsky.

"We've never had anything on this plateau—a gourmet dinner," Mr. Kotimsky said. "So I contributed the services of my rabbi, and I thought he'd be flexible. Suddenly my rabbi says he'll stop the meal. I called my colleagues, and I can't speak for these fellows, and I'm not going to say anything detrimental, but they said they were withdrawing."

He also called Dr. Martin R. Katz, a cardiologist whose favorite organ is not the heart but the stomach, and who had arranged the benefit. To entice gourmets to pay $100, and despite the fact that Israel produces some of the finest Israeli wines in the world, Dr. Katz had promised that the wines would not be kosher.

Arno Schmidt, team advisor and the Waldorf's executive chef, defying the possibility of antitrust prosecution, had earlier gathered the rival caterers in his office, and now he wondered if it had all been in vain. Long distance and short distance, caterers subsequently warned that if clients heard they had attended a dinner with nonkosher wines, business would be ruined.

Meanwhile, team chefs—none is Jewish—were gathering under the eye of Rabbi Shoretz: Franz Eichenauer of General Foods, Gerold K. Berger of Marriott's Essex House, Claude Baills of George Lang, Sture Anderson of the Pinehurst Hotel in North Carolina. Last to arrive was Latzi Wittenberg of Continental Hosts, the team manager.

The reception began with calves' feet à la mode de Caen, salmon en croûte, and four soups in pots—Negev almond chicken soup, Minsk beef borsht, Frankfurt cabbage purée

("I thought about the Rothschilds, who came from Frankfurt," explained Chef Schmidt) and Santander fish *caldo* ("I thought about the Jews in Santander").

Sipping suspiciously, caterers exchanged last-minute intelligence. As Nathan Trotzky approached, Mr. Kotimsky greeted him exuberantly: "Nate, you look thirty years older."

Mr. Trotzky was pleased. "Trotzky," he said. "Dean of them all."

As the one hundred guests entered the Empire Room, they found a menu of wonders undreamed of in Mosaic law: bouquet Imperial Valley on pastry shells shaped like the Star of David; Atlantic striped bass Ambassador, in honor of one of Mr. Bienstock's establishments; granite of apple and cranberry à la Sidney, for Mr. Kotimsky; veal and sweetbreads Leventhal, for Newman & Leventhal; breast of squab Victor, for Victor Mayer; pineapple and crunchy caramel anonymous, understandably; pistachio cake Stanley, for Mr. Lewin; and Sammy's sabayon, for Sammy Jay. (He works for Mr. Mayer.)

The master of ceremonies rose to say he had bad news and good news. The bad news was that all the dinner wines had to be kosher. The good news was that bottles of the promised fine French and Italian wines would be given out as guests left.

Osher of the Waldorf, leaning against the walls of Empire, could hardly contain himself. "You see that?" he asked triumphantly. "You see that? Everybody talks now about kosher wine."

The Kosher
Big Four

THEIR NOTES are not always diplomatic, but when it comes to world-shaking decisions, the Kosher Big Four are in a class of their own. Superpowers of occult learning, large ambition and no small measure of ingenuity, they supervise the rule of dietary law and daily put their authority on the line that says "kosher." With that single word they bring joy to industry and consumer; with the other word—*trayf*, nonkosher—they sow turmoil and despair.

Though they are all based in the New York area, a region that the head of New York State's kosher law enforcement bureau calls "a Mecca for the entire country," there never has been a group photograph of the Big Four. How could there be? While Rabbi Bernard Levy is flying off to Singapore to monitor the refining of palm oil, Rabbi Jacob Cohen follows tea bags moving along an assembly line in Savannah as Rabbi Jehoseph H. Ralbag wanders through California watching fruit ripen at the same time that Rabbi Yacov Lipschutz, representing the hierarchy of the Union of Orthodox Jewish Congregations of America, visits Pittsburgh on the hunt for pickles in a barrel.

These are not men to cavil at the prospect of more flight time than a secretary of state, and it takes more than turbulence aloft and intransigence below to discourage them from extending the dominion of kosher. But the notion of a summit conference was quickly dismissed, characteristically with a question. "Where would we hold it?" Rabbi Lipschutz asked. Who, indeed, would be allowed to supervise the catering?

If there were only four, it would be impossible enough. But these are not the only rabbis in what has been called a billion-dollar business. They are not even the only ones with claims to superpower status in a world where rank is difficult to maintain and impossible to verify. Any rabbi may decide to exercise kosher supervision and aim for the heights, though rare is the expert so favored by fortune that he breaks through from parochial to national, even planetary hegemony.

• • •

A thousand angels can dance on the head of a pin, but the laws of *kashrut*—what is kosher, or permitted—could hardly fit into the heads of a thousand angels.

The Bible proliferates both permissions and prohibitions. In Genesis there is a ban on consuming flesh from a living animal, as well as the sinew of an animal's hip. "Thou shalt not eat any abominable thing," Deuteronomy commands, and Leviticus enumerates a bestiary of the forbidden that includes camel, hare, swine, eagle, vulture, raven, owl, hawk, cuckoo, swan, pelican, cormorant, stork, heron, lapwing, and bat.

Such Biblical injunctions are simplicity compared with

the superstructure in Mishnah and Gemara, the laws and commentary of the Talmud. Here solons and exegetes give exuberant rein to their passion for eliminating frivolities of chance by increasing the complexity of law, giving ready pretexts for calling Mishnah impossible and Gemara irrational.

Deuteronomy allows one to take eggs or young from a nest, but specifies that the mother sitting upon the young or upon the eggs must not be taken. When Mishnah deals with such straightforward raw materials, it spins exceeding fine:

"If the dam hovered over the nest and her wings touched the nest, a man must let her go. . . . A man may not take the dam and her young even for the sake of cleansing the leper."

"They may cover [splashings of blood and blood that remains on the knife] with fine dung or with fine sand, with lime, or with [pieces of] potsherd or a brick or the plug of a jar that have been crushed; but they may not cover it up with coarse dung or coarse sand, or with a brick or a plug that have not been crushed, nor may they set over it a vessel turned upside down." Some texts add: "or cover it with stone."

Mishnah meticulously details accidents rendering cattle *trayf;* e.g., "If the gullet is pierced; or if the heart is pierced as far as the cells thereof; or if the spine is broken and the spinal cord severed; or if the liver is gone and naught soever of it remains . . ." Maimonides, the twelfth-century sage, itemized seventy defects and diseases, and listed these sinister bars under headings such as: mauled by wild animals or birds, fallen and thus suspected of suffering shock and damage, torn, split, broken.

Though some attempt to explain dietary laws as ancient

hygiene, others suggest that the laws encourage obedience, self-discipline and thus sanctity. An observant Jew is denied innumerable pleasures of the palate because of their danger to the soul—lobsters, ham, even sirloin steak unless the forbidden sciatic nerve is removed. Many Jews obey none of the ancient dietary laws, while others adjust compliance to please themselves, eating ham, for example, but not lobsters, or lobsters but not ham, or mixing milk and meat, or eating off plates used for both milk and meat—as long as no nonkosher meat is served.

Even modern guides to *kashrut* hardly make life easier. In the handbook of the Union of Orthodox Jewish Congregations, some eight hundred bodies often referred to collectively as the U, true believers are advised that rabbis should be consulted about dishwashers used for both meat and dairy dishes, and that even in pet food one should avoid cooked products containing milk combined with beef, veal or mutton.

• • •

Rabbi Levy has been almost sixty years in this world, fifteen years in the kosher business. He has the sinews of a young man and the black beard of a patriarch. At home in Brooklyn he has a filing cabinet burgeoning with kosher correspondence, but the letters of several millennia seem to have migrated onto his desk. He sits slumped behind the clutter, comforted by signs proclaiming that clearheadedness is worth a mess. The *rebbetzin,* the rabbi's wife, is in charge of filing, and her husband calls her "boss."

Logging an annual total he estimates as "millions of miles," he spends about three-quarters of the year traveling, and much of the rest in jet lag. As he nods over his desk's stratified burden, his mind is lulled by memories of distant chores. He has just returned from West Germany, where he looked into the production of kosher cysteine hydrochloride made from Chinese hair provided by cooperative barbers. The chemical is used in surgery and intravenous feeding, and as an agent that makes bread rise and increases the viscosity of dough. It also lends a flavor of meat.

Rabbi Levy stopped in Denmark to check on cheese, and in The Netherlands to inspect cookies. "A Dutch firm wants to break into the American kosher market," the rabbi says, "but it's going to take a little effort." He thinks back also to his efforts in Japan (rennet), Taiwan (mushrooms), Spain (olive oil), England (sweets), Portugal (sardines), Italy (vitamins), and Belgium (chocolates). "I have Wesson oil, I have Sunkist, I have canneries," he says. "Hunt's wanted to use bacon in some products, and use the same equipment for canned kosher potatoes. I wouldn't certify it." Anaconda wanted approval for aluminum foil—the problem was the lubricant used in manufacture. Rabbi Levy approved. When McCormick insisted he get advance permission each time he wanted to check on a spice factory, he withdrew his services and published the correspondence attesting to his principled refusal. In kosher matters, as far as Rabbi Levy is concerned, who knows if McCormick is still the real McCoy?

When the phone rings, the rabbi is occasionally available to answer. "What is this?" he asks his caller. "A chopped liver? . . . Chicken? . . . Where you going to make it? . . . In Weinberg's plant? . . . But it's not a telephone conversation. You can come over and we can discuss it."

Rabbi Levy entered the field of long- and short-distance expertise to help an aging rabbi. "Before you knew it I got involved in it," he says, "and this became my main occupation." Before anyone else knew it, be became a conglomerate, operating as Organized Kashrut (O.K.) Laboratories, which has a postal box but no chemist; he also became prime mover in the Committee for the Furtherance of Torah Observance, which shares the box. O.K. and C.F.T.O. together—in any case, it's hard to keep them apart—publish *The Jewish Homemaker incorporating the kosher food guide*. The kosher food guide lists those whose fidelity to dietary law he supervises, who display on their merchandise his K seal and sometimes simply his peremptory K, an initial also used by others. His products include Barricini candy, Grape-Nuts, Maxwell House coffee, Philadelphia cream cheese, Log Cabin syrup and Sam's *knishes*. The bimonthly *Homemaker* brings the latest news in what it terms the kosher crisis; e.g., joyous tidings that the Lubavitcher Rebbe will pay 50 percent of the cost of dishes, pots and cutlery—in fact, everything needed to make a home kosher. Sometimes the word is cautionary: the magazine warns that if a man eats "crass and debased foods, the workings of his mind will tend to be likewise crass, debased and dulled."

An annual subscription costs $3, and for services to food companies Rabbi Levy usually gets $750 to $1,200 a year. A large company may have to pay as much as $40,000.

Like others who practice kosher supervision, Rabbi Levy daily runs the risk of conflict of interests. His guiding principles should be the public weal and the law's demands, but those who pay him are the manufacturer, the hotel, the caterer. It takes uncommon firmness to avoid shortchanging the public while boosting his income and his favor with clients. In Europe, classically, *kashrut* supervisors were employed by the community. Their independence was easier to assure.

As kosher lines expand, so do the opportunities. Rabbi Levy has therefore converted his domain into a tri-rabbi area, employing his son Rabbi Daniel Levy and Rabbi Zvi

M. Gartenhaus of Flatbush. There are about seventy others, subcontractors of a sort, who operate under the wing of Levy *père*. For those who need all-day supervision, he provides *mashgichim*, on-the-spot kosher watchmen.

Another rabbi might stay at home and watch the fees roll in, but Rabbi Levy's course is onward and upward. "I'm a nervous guy," he says. "I'm restless. I'm worried. I don't trust anybody. There are questions you don't have answers to, so you're stringent. Some people make a nice living from certifications I turn down." When the question appears unfathomable, he goes right to the top and submits it to Rabbi Moshe Feinstein, the Lower East Side's most celebrated expert on difficult questions of religious law. Rabbi Feinstein ponders precedents, pierces mysteries, and writes opinions known as Responsa.

There was the sensitive question of Milait, a product made from an enzyme taken from the tongue of an animal. "It gives a cow-y taste," the rabbi says. "I knew it could be kosher, but I didn't want to take it on my own shoulders. So I went to Rabbi Feinstein, and he agreed it could be kosher. To extract the enzyme, the tongues should not be put in milk, since milk is a milk product and meat should not be mixed with milk. But if it's cooked in whey it's all right. Whey is not a milk product according to the Bible; it's only milk for the rabbinical sages."

To the suggestion that this is casuistry, splitting hairs, Rabbi Levy counters: "That's what Responsa are. That's what lawyers do all day long. That's what rabbis do. That's their interpretation of Jewish law."

He has now given his blessing to the whey of five different companies, and in this fivefold whey the production of enzymes could suffice to assure the demand of the entire Western Hemisphere, including offshore islands.

Occasionally, Rabbi Levy is so enamored of a product

that he gives it a special blessing, as he has done for Mr. Gefilte Fish. When Rabbi Feinstein heard that Mr. Gefilte Fish was selling so much that the plant *mashgiach* could not inspect all the fish, the sage of the Lower East Side demanded additional *mashgichim,* and the company promptly complied. In Rabbi Levy's experience, such corporate collaboration in the kosher cause is in the highest traditions. He is also high on fully breaded, fully cooked Essen fried chicken.

What he is low on is sympathy for competitors who try to steal business. Those rabbis who solicit accounts he warns of *chillul Hashem* (profanation of God's name) and *hassogas g'vul* (poaching on another's preserves). "There are doctors and doctors, lawyers and lawyers, rabbis and rabbis," he says. "A rabbi's a human being. He's got weaknesses. It's an unfortunate situation. There's nothing I can do about it except cry."

• • •

Rabbi Cohen remembers his father answering questions at home about chickens. "Then Breakstone came to him. They said, 'Rabbi, we need a rabbi.' So my father became the rabbi of Breakstone cheese, and I took over from him eventually. He was also the rabbi of Swee-touch-nee tea, on Division Street, and got $55 for supervising them during all of Passover. 'Tutteh [father],' I said to him, 'I wouldn't do it for $55.'"

His father sent him to Palestine and then to Poland to study at famous rabbinical academies, and he wondered if the trips were necessary: "What did I need to be a rabbi? Learn how to speak well, learn a little bit of Talmud, learn a little bit of Torah."

In Poland, however, he discovered the blessed intricacies of *kashrut.* "I studied the first volume—slaughtering. If you want to be a rabbi, you have to know how a *shoichet* slaughters. Number 2 is the laws of *trayfus*—what is forbidden. Three is the laws of mixing milk and meat, 4 the laws of blood—which you can eat and can't eat—5 the laws of fats. A rabbi has to know what's the lung, what's the stomach. It interested me to know the details. It's a very deep study. If the animal has a broken leg or a broken arm, if it has a crossed eye or a wart, it's *trayf.* I had to learn if a blemish will fade away. Rav, in the Talmud, is asked how he became an expert on sheep. He says, 'I went to a shepherd, a plain shepherd who tends his sheep. I was with him for eighteen years.' He was buddy-buddy. So a rabbi learns. He should know religion, philosophy; he should know holidays—Sukkos and Shavuos and Rosh haShanah. But where does he come to *kashrut?* Rav spent time there, and I spent thirty-five years in the profession. I acquired experience and knowledge. In the beginning I just had cheese.

"When it came into shortening and emulsifiers and other ingredients, first of all I looked to see if there was an endorsement. In those days it had, say, Ⓤ. If it didn't have an endorsement, I would ask the chemist at the plant what was in the product. Or I would sit down with a friend from my synagogue, a chemist, and ask him. What are we looking for? We're looking for it should not be an animal ingredient, it shouldn't be *trayf.* I got to know it by study, from the analysis."

Recently, Rabbi Cohen was summoned to a cookie company, and he noted after his inspection: "The margarine has a K. The shortening is Ⓤ. The eggs—they have to be supervised to see there isn't blood—that's Ⓤ. Wilbur's chocolate—I know the rabbi; he's the one from the chocolate at Barton's. Nestlé's chocolate—he happens to be Rabbi Ralbag, a reliable man. Then I put down other ingredients. Salt—I'm not worried about it. The sugar is all right. The flour—it's pure flour in the bags. And then I put down 'No gelatin in the plant.' I want only the kosher ingredients we planned for. Every company knows that any ingredient they want to add, I can pass on it."

Cottage cheese has been a running problem. "It comes from milk," Rabbi Cohen says. "So that is the crux of the dairy inspection, because cottage cheese, to make it firm, has to use a starter, and the starter is rennet. According to the Talmud, rennet comes from the stomach of calves. So how would we use it for cheese? The answer is, rennet is the juice taken out of the calves' stomach. They take the organ and they dry it on the sun for thirty days, and it becomes like a piece of wood. So it lost its strength of dairy or anything. This is a fact, like *Baruch atah adonai* [Blessed art Thou, O Lord our God]."

At Passover, corn is a plague all by itself. "The whole restriction of Passover is between leavened and unleavened—bread and matzoh," the rabbi says. "When a lady would grind down the corn, it would have the look of flour. The lady next door would see it and say it's *chometz* [not kosher for Passover]. Some companies during the sugar emergency used corn syrup during Passover. On such a problem I would ask Moshe Feinstein. There's even a permissible mixture of milk and meat; a tiny bit—a sixtieth part—of milk with meat is all right. But *chometz* shouldn't fly in. There shouldn't be a speck."

Passover is the busiest season, and as though a seventy-year-old rabbi had spare time on his hands, Tetley still insists on having its tea produced under rabbinical supervision. When Rabbi Cohen is asked why tea needs supervision, he replies: "I was wondering about that, too." He suggests that the producer is perhaps eager to have the label proclaiming supervision for Passover.

When he gets a written inquiry, Rabbi Cohen makes a point of expressing modesty. "A rabbi has to be humble," he says. "He doesn't have to ring the bell." So in replying he writes, "For the one who wishes to know," as though offering his opinion under duress.

He is now an expert not only in *kashrut* but in airline schedules, and in New Jersey and New York State he can draw road maps from memory, so great are his wanderings, so recurrent his visits. "Certain companies we had thirty, thirty-five years ago, we usually raise the prices slowly," he said. "I wouldn't go under $400, $500 on anything. But big companies that become affiliated with me, so you get a few thousand dollars. Most of my work is devoted to *kashrut.* My *shul* in Spring Valley is not one I would devote myself to like I was a youngster. I have somebody to help me. I tell my children, 'What can I do? Daddy works because he likes it. If you are so interested as I am, you won't feel old when you work.'

"The Almighty gave me the privilege of doing this work. That was what the Almighty wanted. So I have something much more important than fee—that's to perfect your *kashrut*, that your products should be pure. My people, when they see at the supermarket a product under my supervision—I'm the letter K on my products—it's a challenge to me; it's a prize that gives me great pleasure, to service them. To them it's their whole life, and that gives me the impetus, gives me the strength, gives me the excitement, gives me the feeling and interest to do it."

• • •

Rabbi Ralbag bestrides the city like a colossus, with one synagogue, Bnai Israel, on the East Side and another, Ramath Orah, on the West Side. "One Shabbas here and one Shabbas there," he says.

He lives in the same apartment building on West 86th Street as Isaac Bashevis Singer, and across the street is a bakery that makes shtrudel like they used to make in the old country. But even a situation this idyllic is not enough to satisfy Rabbi Ralbag—or Mr. Singer, for that matter. The Nobel Prize–winning author is forever running off to give lectures on the oi's of Yiddish, and Rabbi Ralbag is perpetually en route to and from airports to investigate the wheys of *kashrut*. "At least once a year I'm in every place," he said. "I have rabbis in areas—in the dozens, say more than a dozen. But I have to see what's happening. I want to make a spot inspection. Some things, it's enough to be there once in a while. You don't have to be in orange juice every day in the year, because it's just orange juice. But in a sausage factory you have to be there from day to night. Maybe in a restaurant you have to be there. What if some nonkosher meat comes in? Who's going to watch over it? God is going to watch over it?"

Rabbi Ralbag speaks with the vivacity of seltzer shpritzing from a bottle, and somewhere or other he has discovered the fountain of youth. When asked his age, he bobs and weaves and finally blurts, "I'm about sixty-four, I think," quickly adding: "In Judaism, age is experience."

In the first flower of his youth he served a *kashrut* apprenticeship in the Bronx, every Thursday submitting to an inundation of chickens brought by housewives who wanted his assurance that the birds were kosher. Then, about forty years ago, the rabbi who supervised *kashrut* for Borden's threatened to succumb beneath a flood of sour cream and cried for help. A *kashrut* star was born.

"I became known," Rabbi Ralbag says. "My certificates were accepted nationally or internationally. There are greater scholars than me and less important scholars than me. I am to a certain extent an authority on Jewish law. I have the holy books and I weigh the pros and cons and I do it with a very weighty mind. If you're not an authority and just say a thing is not kosher, that's not a big deal. Jewish law is very profound. It doesn't end with itself.

"There are two things I feel are very important. Number one is that the rabbi who certifies the product—I don't want to use the term 'Orthodox'; I believe Jews are Jews—but I believe I'm a hundred percent observant, so the rabbi has to be an observant man. A rabbi who isn't observant can't give kosher certification. But you have to know Jewish law, especially as it involves itself with modern technology. A rabbi must be the one to give certification. A chemist can't give certification. If he makes a mistake, how is he going to know? God is going to tell him? If you don't give a rap for the laws, you shouldn't be a judge. Law means interpretation. If a person doesn't believe in it, he's not going to give you a correct interpretation."

Rabbi Ralbag is still bubbling away as he replies to the insistent jangle of the phone in his study. Someone has received a frozen concentrated cranberry juice with the name Welch on it, though it's distributed by Ocean Spray—or so it seems. "Ocean Spray is under my certification," the rabbi says. "Welch is a problem. Welch makes grape juice. Grape juice is different from other fruits and vegetables, which are kosher. When it comes to grape juice, it comes under a sacramental problem. The very moment a grape is squeezed, technically it's sacramental. So it comes under the category of kosher wine." He stops for breath and adds: "Ocean Spray, all of a sudden! If I see they're making grape juice I'll start raising Cain."

Conservative Jews have been told by their law committee that all wine is kosher—advice heretical by Orthodox standards. For the Orthodox, only if Jews have made the wine is it kosher. Rabbi Ralbag explains that the distinction about wine arose because wine could lead to conviviality, to put it mildly, and intermarriage, to put it bluntly.

When the phone rings again, it is the Beich Candy Company of Illinois. Rabbi Ralbag can hardly believe his ears. "There is no such thing as subkosher," he tells his caller. "It's either kosher or not kosher."

As soon as he hangs up, the phone rings again, and this time the call is from a company that makes commercial baking mixes. The company has one plant in upstate New York, where production is nonkosher, and another plant in Chicago, where everything is kosher. By mistake, some mix from New York landed in a kosher bakery where Rabbi Ralbag has a *mashgiach*, and the product did not go down well with this vigilant guardian of the law. The mix did not have either of the rabbi's seals—a K, or for those who prefer an insignia more distinctive, a Ⓚ. And the descriptive code on the container was in black, not the red that the rabbi specified. "He can see it," Rabbi Ralbag says of his *mashgiach*. "He's got vision. He saw it wasn't what my letter states. It was a black code. He's doing what I told him to do. I said, 'You did the right thing, and it's important to watch.'

"I want to be responsible. God forbid it should go wrong and God forbid it should be bad for me. My companies have my identity, and I'm responsible. If Rabbi Ralbag, God forbid, like Nixon gets destroyed, the government survives, the organization survives, *kashrut* survives."

When the phone is silent, trouble comes in the door. A new magazine, *Kosher Home*, mistakenly listed Nestlé's semisweet morsels as kosher and dairy, though Rabbi Ralbag had certified the delicacy as kosher and *pareve*. Rabbis and housewives have been writing from all over the country. "I had to get a person to answer the hundreds of letters," Rabbi Ralbag complains proudly. "Nestlé said to me, 'Now we see that your word counts.' They got letters from all over the country. Europe didn't come yet."

Rabbi Ralbag certifies products for a dazzling assortment of companies, including Standard Brands, Coca-Cola, General Mills and General Foods, but he has had to give up some certifications. "I don't mind competition, because I feel unfortunately, since there's a fee involved, there are rabbis who come up once in a while who feel, 'Why should Rabbi Ralbag give certifications? I can give them.' To me, I'm not worried. Kosher is a thing that has to do with religion. If somebody says he can give a certification, what can you do? Father Divine said he was God, so what are you going to do about it?

"Fee depends. From a few hundred dollars to a few thousand. By me, fee is not important. When General Foods has kosher, when Bird's Eye has kosher on their vegetables or Drake has kosher on their cakes, the fee is the smallest thing. I don't want to mention names. But say Nabisco. It doesn't have kosher on their cakes and it's a huge business. If a company goes to the trouble of getting kosher ingredients, the fee is the smallest thing. I tell that to the U. 'Don't feel that you're big shots. If they go to the trouble of making kosher, why give them exorbitant fees?'

"The U is a layman's organization. There are some synagogues in the U that are not a hundred percent—they have mixed pews. But they have a division where they take care of kosher. Now this division has rabbis and probably laymen, too, to take care of their kosher certification. I don't like to knock other rabbis. I say I don't care who gives certification. I want more people to eat kosher. Of course, certain plants I don't supervise anymore. They got other rabbis. I never said my certificate is better than theirs, although it is."

• • •

Rabbi Lipschutz is rabbinic coordinator for *kashrut* of the Union of Orthodox Jewish Congregations, which is affiliated with the Rabbinical Council of America. The *kashrut* division goes back to the twenties; but Rabbi Lipschutz, a spring chicken who hails from New England, goes back only to 1932, give or take a bob or weave.

"There have been great changes in American industry," he notes. "World War II taught America to produce all-vegetable shortening, synthetics became widespread, marketing became different—supermarkets instead of mom-and-pop stores. Leading companies became aware there was a mass Jewish market. The mentality of the producer changed. Thanks to the government, he knows what it is to be supervised.

"You have a very competitive field. Nucoa margarine or Mazola cannot sell for more than anyone else. We want to create the atmosphere where a kosher product won't cost more. *Kashrut* is not a tax on the item. Per product it costs only millicents, and companies do it not to satisfy the Jews but to sell the products. Most products that we certify *require* certification. If it's glycerine it has to be synthetic. If it's vegetable oil it has to be produced in a plant that produces only vegetable oil. People may be vegetarian and not realize that they're brushing their teeth with animal products. Due to our success there are companies who feel that our Ⓤ symbol would be to their advantage, even though we may feel it's an innocent product. So we cannot say to them, 'No, we will not give it to you.'"

Rabbi Lipschutz wavers back and forth on whether

once-a-year inspection could ever be enough: "It may be enough. . . . It's not right. . . . Take plastic dishes. I think as a matter of course, in order to maintain the proper posture in the eyes of the company, we would say quarterly or biannually. Not that you suspect anything. . . . Each case is unique. We have places where we have five, six men at a time. Take the Cross Brothers slaughterhouse in Philadelphia. Or Horowitz matzohs, where we have five *mashgichim*. . . . We have hotels and caterers and factories, and we are like a depository of *kashrut* information for all over the world. We have emulsifiers in Sweden and Denmark, even as far as Japan; herring fillets in Sweden; sardines in Norway and Portugal. The more complicated the problem, the more I thrive on it. Now we've even produced for the first time sherry wine in Spain."

The Union is supreme in poultry, where it supervises Empire, Falls, Moriah and Levin Brothers. Kosher poultry is more expensive than nonkosher, and Rabbi Lipschutz has a short-order explanation: "If you would enter a nonkosher plant, the chicken is put down into a machine and zippo— it's a razor blade, and it goes pop, pop, pop, knocks off the heads. Automatically it's put in hot water and scalded to get the feathers off, it's eviscerated, and in no time at all it's in a plastic bag and blast-frozen, almost with no manpower on the whole assembly line.

"Now take a kosher plant. When the birds come in, each one has to be handed in person to a *shoichet* to be killed by hand, so you have five or six or eight on a line. The biggest advance that you have in *kashrut* is that you have cold-water plucking machines, but they do not get rid of the pinfeathers. The machines tear the skin sometimes, so those birds have to be sold at lower prices. And the men on the line are not slave labor. That's $2.65 government minimum, and some of them are union shops. Then you have inspectors and *mashgichim* who have to examine the intestines of every bird. The bird may be nonkosher because of perforations. So they'll take away from you, say, three out of a hundred; that's thirty out of a thousand. And that's just the start. You have to have equipment in which the bird soaks for a half hour. Then the birds have to dry off and be salted inside and out. That requires salters and supervisors. The salt costs money; it's not free. The people on the line cost something. It has to be in the salt for an hour. So it's already two hours and that bird's not done yet. He's still floating around, and then he has to be rinsed off. Then he can move to the assembly line to be packed. The pure economics of this country are such that if you want kosher, the bird has to cost more."

Sometimes Rabbi Lipschutz considers how terrible life would be without organized *kashrut* inspection. Modern American women would not stand in line waiting for a man to pluck feathers; more and more Jews would sink to eating *trayf*, slipping into perdition mouthful by mouthful. But now the trend seems to be not toward *trayf* but toward *glatt*, a word that has come to suggest super-pure, as though there were degrees of kosher. "You have to appreciate the American way of life," Rabbi Lipschutz says. "It's come to mean better, the best, perfect.

"Any blemish on the lungs of a bird, the bird is *trayf*, but if it's an animal, not a bird, it may be kosher even with a blemish. In the United States, thank God, it doesn't exist, chickens with diseased lungs. Intestines, yes. Ulcers, growths, sometimes swollen heads. A *shoichet* will touch the head once in a while to check.

"If it's an animal, after you *shoicht* [slaughter], you open it up and put your hand in the cavity and feel the lungs. Where there's a perforation, there's an adhesion. They'll take off the adhesion and put the lung on a table and pump

it up like an inner tube, and if it bubbles, there's a perforation, which means the animal is *trayf.* "

Rabbi Lipschutz, who readily separates animals into
kosher and nonkosher, likes to say there is no such person
as a Conservative Jew or a Reform Jew. "I believe that all
Jews should feel for their faith," he says. To the suggestion
that many Jews reject fidelity to orthodoxy and to the rules
and apparatus of *kashrut,* he responds: "I know. Where do
you think I grew up—by the Wailing Wall? Some of my
best friends say that."

Law Enforcement in the Kosher Line

WEEKENDS, Rabbi Schulem Rubin leads his Bronx congregation in prayer, drawing their thoughts to rewards of the afterlife. The rest of the week he leads a squad of law enforcement inspectors, directing their attention to penalties of the here and now. In the New York State Department of Agriculture and Markets, he heads the kosher law enforcement bureau. The law requires truth in labeling and in advertising, and Rabbi Rubin's job is to protect the consumer from misrepresentation and fraud in the kosher line. He is a David contending with a Goliath industry that does an estimated billion dollars of business a year, much of it in New York. "For kosher things, New York is a Mecca for the entire country," Rabbi Rubin says.

Solid of body and stalwart of spirit, he seems equal to every challenge; only his hair, grown white, suggests that in his five decades he has known trials as well as triumphs.

In his many years in the department he has grown not only older—he was prepared for that—but sadder, when he thinks about violations of laws that have the double force of secular mandate and sacred rite. "We're getting in-depth violations that we never got before," he said. "The situation is chaotic, without question."

Rabbi Rubin entered state employ in 1975 as field supervisor and quickly distinguished himself by solving the case of the hot chickens.

"If you put a chicken into hot water to make the skin smooth and attractive, it's not kosher," he said. "And how hot is too hot? The Talmud says that it's as long as it takes for your finger to burn.

"We suspected a very big producer of kosher chickens, but whenever our inspectors arrived the water was cold, and whenever our inspectors left the water was hot. So how did they do it? They delayed the inspectors at the entrance while they chilled the water. But I rushed in with a calibrated thermometer, and the water was 120 degrees. If you put your finger in 120 degrees you begin to feel it, and the chicken feels it too. I caught them red-handed. Within minutes the whole chicken operation ceased—it was such a shock. I broke that case, and it made me a sort of hero, although it didn't take much genius or great surveillance. The inspector who was with me told me our lives were in danger."

When the job as head of kosher enforcement opened up, hot endorsements of Rabbi Rubin flooded into the governor's office from all manner of Jewish organizations. After a while he got a call from the governor's office. "Enough!" the official said. "No more letters."

Rabbi Rubin got the job. The original head of the bureau had been there forty years, pioneering in the struggle; he had had enough trouble without looking for more. But Rabbi Rubin decided he would go after well-known institutions that were supposed to be kosher: if he found them guilty of fraud he would act. "No sacred cows," he said. "I don't care how much political clout they have. If they're breaking the law, they'll go on the chopping block. And if they go after me and find skeletons in my past, the skeletons will be of wax and they'll melt with the heat of the truth."

Just before the rabbi's first Thanksgiving as head of the bureau, one of his inspectors descended on a hotel in the Catskills that advertises itself as kosher and found about a hundred nonkosher Swift's Butterball turkeys. They were for the staff, management said, but possession of nonkosher items is sufficient for a penalty. Word of Operation Turkey quickly spread, and the results were dramatic. "The next Thanksgiving you couldn't find a single Swift Butterball turkey flying around a Catskills hotel," Rabbi Rubin said.

When he addressed a meeting of the Catskills Resort Association, he said he would continue to enforce the law. Individually and collectively the members threatened resistance, arguing that the department had treated them with deference during forty years. Department records indicate that this is true, though as Rabbi Rubin was to write in an official report, "It is very hard to believe that a Swift's Butterball turkey found its way there for the first time in forty years."

"We have enough clout to disintegrate your department and put you out of business," Rabbi Rubin remembers a hotel owner saying to him. " 'This isn't forty years ago,' I replied. 'You're not going to put us out of business.' "

He recalls another owner saying: "We have enough trouble with Environment, with Health, and now we have you to worry about. Be careful how you step off the curb. Remember, your predecessor was hit by a car when he stepped off a curb."

"I didn't know if he was threatening me or joking," Rabbi Rubin said. "If I were a nervous Nellie, I'd be worried."

Judah Gribetz, the governor's counsel, summoned Rabbi Rubin and heard his version of the Catskills saga. "If you do anything but what you are doing, then *you're* wrong," he remembers Mr. Gribetz saying to him. While Rabbi Rubin was there, Governor Carey came in and spoke privately to his counsel. It may have been about kosher matters, but maybe it wasn't. "I'm sure he has more important things to do than look for a chicken flicker," Rabbi Rubin suggested.

Buoyed by official support, the rabbi pressed his eleven inspectors to be industrious and vigilant. But with some twenty-one thousand inspections to make each year, the staff has no time for twenty-three of the state's sixty-two counties. A sample of violations suggests that the only foolproof defense—other than compliance—is migration to one of those twenty-three:

• At a kosher meat market in Oceanside, New York, an inspector reported what Rabbi Rubin called "a serious, unpardonable violation." "We found the owner playing around with chickens," he said, "fraudulently mislabeling and deceptively misrepresenting." The kosher law bureau says that the birds were "Cookin' Good" nonkosher chickens; loosely attached to their wings were kosher tags taken from kosher chickens.

• At a restaurant in Queens, New York, inspectors acting on a tip seized six ducks. The ducks were analyzed by specialists in kosher ducks: the joint near the webbed foot had none of the yellow or orange skin that adheres to a kosher duck, and the outer epidermis had been removed by scalding, probably with hot wax—strictly not kosher. Serious, wanton, unpardonable infraction, Rabbi Rubin ruled, noting that the owner had "violated the trust of his kosher consumers."

A hotel in Woodbourne, New York, had seven boxes of Maryland Quick Frozen Bite-Size Sea Nuggets containing clams, shrimp and crabmeat, all of which are nonkosher. The hotel steward said the Nuggets were for the staff, but in any case heating nonkosher food in kosher utensils renders the utensils nonkosher.

• In South Fallsburg, New York, a hotel had lumpfish caviar, which is not kosher, and milk in the breading used for veal cutlets. Following the dictates of Exodus and Deuteronomy, milk products must not be cooked or consumed with meat.

• During Passover, yet another hotel in South Fallsburg had products not kosher for Passover—Avanti mozzarella, Roma Bouquet Romano cheese, Maggi seasoning, Fry cooking oil.

• A supermarket in Elmont, New York, included nonkosher chicken fat in the section marked kosher, to wit eight containers of Mrs. Kornberg's *shmaltz*.

"I myself have gone out to Borough Park, the Jerusalem of America, and written out a violation," Rabbi Rubin said. By law the label on prepacked kosher meat must indicate whether the meat was "soaked and salted." To be kosher, liver must be broiled, not soaked and salted. But in Borough Park the liver had a label declaring "soaked and salted." So, as Rabbi Rubin said, "If he did soak and salt, it's *trayf*—nonkosher; and if he didn't soak and salt, it's not truth in labeling."

"When a man sits there with a yarmulke and puts on a pious appearance, I think he has a great responsibility," the rabbi said. "Some people would get sick if they ate 'kosher' food and found they were in the process of digesting non-kosher food. They'd get physically sick."

Rabbi Rubin's writ runs not only to establishments within New York State but also to any which advertise in New York that they are "under rabbinical supervision." They must specify the name of the rabbi, and Rabbi Rubin has been demanding compliance as far south as Miami Beach.

To excuse transgressions, violators sometimes suggest that they're Conservative kosher, or Reform kosher, but as far as Rabbi Rubin is concerned, there's no such thing: kosher is kosher. "I'm not an inspector of rabbis," he said. "I'm not interested in the qualifications of the rabbi but in the truth of the label."

His duties have been complicated by the vogue for glatt—or super-kosher. Glatt means smooth, but strictly speaking the term is applied to an animal with no blemish on the lungs. Rabbi Rubin becomes immediately suspicious when told that 90 percent of a random herd are glatt kosher. "Something's wrong, unless they have the angel Gabriel working for them," he said. "If there's an inflation of glatt, then something isn't kosher. But today there are even nightclubs that call themselves glatt—with glatt belly dancers." One violator caught mixing milk and meat protested to Rabbi Rubin: "I never told you we were glatt kosher. We're just kosher."

The department issues thousands of "warnings"—less severe than "violations"—and hardly any hotels in the Catskills remain unscathed. "I'm not a meter maid who's trying to give out more and more tickets," Rabbi Rubin protested. "Sometimes I feel sorry for the offenders. I don't go for indictments. This should be reserved for those who rob and murder and kill. If a man goes to jail even for five minutes, it's not child's play. But I have to protect the public. If somebody simply, directly, clearly, sells non-kosher as kosher, then I'll be cruel; I'll be mean. One of these days we'll find a caterer or butcher in such violation that he'll have to go out of business."

When the Oceanside case was discovered, Rabbi Rubin called inspectors together in his office on the fiftieth floor of the World Trade Center and asked what to do about the butcher. Their reply, as he remembers, was simple: "Hang him." Rabbi Rubin accordingly assessed the maximum $200 per violation, which meant 11 chickens times $200, or $2,200.

"Most of the people who deal with kosher food are honest," he said. "I don't consider them as Mafia, if there is such a thing, and I don't consider myself as a prosecutor. If there is a Mafia, they would want somebody like me, who would make sure kosher was kosher.

"To me kosher is a sacred thing, though my duty is not to impose my opinions but to enforce the law. It's exhilarating, nonetheless, to do something that is so close to my soul. I think it's the best thing that ever happened to me. I have no tension here. I have more tension in one weekend at my synagogue than in a week on this job."

Miracle

TRADITIONAL JEWS interpret the Bible as forbidding meat and dairy dishes at the same meal, but instead of resting content with the wisdom of the sages, Ralph Goodman and Heinz Rohr wanted to do something about it. They own The Cake Stylists, of Queens, New York, and they dreamed of producing a cheesecake that was *pareve*—neither meat nor dairy—and thus acceptable at any meal.

Suddenly, like a bolt from heaven, they got a call from a supplier offering a *pareve*, imitation cheese base. "My eyes lit up," said Mr. Goodman.

When he tried making cheesecake with the base, his eyes went dark again.

But the Queens men had kneaded enough dough to sink the *Queen Mary*, so they persevered, tinkering with the base, changing ingredients, braving heat and disappointment. Mornings became evenings, days turned into weeks, months disappeared.

"First it came out too soft," said Horst Schumacher, the plant manager. "We couldn't get enough stability into it—the cakes fell as they came up and fell as they went down. We tried whole eggs, we tried yolks, we tried texturized eggs, we tried combinations."

"It looked like a custard pie, and that we had to avoid under any circumstances," Mr. Rohr said. "It had to entice people. It had to look like a cheesecake."

"We added things, we eliminated things," Mr. Goodman recalled. "It was too thin, too thick, too heavy, too flat. A million and one things went wrong. The stuff we threw out here was unbelievable. I was sick of tasting cheesecake."

Then, on a day that seemed just like any other, Mr. Goodman took one more taste. "By jove," he exclaimed, "we've got it!"

He quickly clamped down a lid of secrecy that the Pentagon would envy, with burglar alarms, security warnings and restricted access. Only four people received cheesecake clearances: the three developers and Mr. Goodman's son Michael, who has a master's degree in urban planning and seems to be working toward a doctorate in kosher pastry. The other employees have been content not to pry, lest they become subject to suborning by foreign spies or by this country's Cheesecake Intelligence Agency.

To ensure that the product remains *pareve* and kosher, Rabbi Moshe Weinberg patrols the bakery relentlessly. When ingredients arrive, he scans them carefully, alert for the slightest infraction. As cakes depart he beams proudly, satisfied that he has upheld the integrity of divine law. When carefully screened visitors try to wheedle secrets out of the solemn rabbi, his is the silence of the grave. "Don't mention names," Mr. Goodman warns.

"I speak about kosher things, not business," the rabbi responds. "As it says in Hebrew, a word to the wise is already plenty."

Kosher caterers—Kotimsky & Tuchman, Newman &

Leventhal, Victor Mayer, Majestic, Jem—have begun buying the cheesecake for their banquets. Gourmands who
enjoy meat dishes and indigestion in perfect compliance
with religious law can now, with a clear conscience, savor
the added bliss of cheesecake for dessert. Some may find it
hard to swallow rabbinical assurances that there is no
cheese in the cheesecake, but they have the word not only
of Rabbi Weinberg but of the entire Union of Orthodox
Jewish Congregations of America, and the symbol—Ⓤ—
conveying that blessing.

"Some kosher caterers were afraid to put it on the table,"
Mr. Rohr said. "The guests were suspicious. Some wouldn't
touch the cheesecake, and some who did touch it wouldn't
touch it again—they thought they'd already committed one
sin."

Abe Lebewohl of the Second Avenue Delicatessen offered the cake to himself night after night before putting it
on his menu and inviting others to share the miracle. "It's a
breakthrough!" cried one client. "Like landing a man on
the moon."

"I can't figure out what's in it," said Blanche Seltzer,
"and I come from a family of bakers."

A wholesale distributor plans to sell the cake to retail
outlets, and Mr. Goodman and Mr. Rohr wonder how their
staff will manage. They are already struggling with a line
rich in mammoth cakes surmounted by edible brides,
grooms, even dolls with flounces. And all this is child's play
alongside the artistic demands posed by the creation each
week of over a hundred Torah-shaped cakes—Torahs open,
Torahs closed—to say nothing of pastry triumphs such as
the Forest Hills tennis club, the Goodyear blimp and—
masterpiece of twenty years' partnership—the Rego Park
Jewish Center.

Having now outdone themselves, the miracle men are

still at a loss for a name. "Pareve-nu" seems too obscure for words. "We're not allowed to call it cheesecake, even though it looks, tastes and smells like it," said Mr. Rohr.

"This one doesn't stick to your mouth, so I like it better than real cheesecake," said Mr. Schumacher.

"With ours you don't get a heavy lump in your stomach," added Mr. Rohr. "We were afraid it would have an after-taste. I have to be honest—it still has a little."

"Such a little," said Mr. Goodman quickly, "it's not worth mentioning."

Grocery

LEIBEL BISTRITSKY'S kosher grocery is at 27½ Essex Street, but he does not believe in half measures. Until 4 P.M. his store is all business. Then business goes out the window and women go out the door: for ten minutes the grocery becomes a place of worship. The store fills with Orthodox Jews who work in the neighborhood, rocking back and forth as they say *mincha*—afternoon prayers. The space between the counter and the wall is just wide enough for a single worshipper.

"It's a two-by-nothing store," said Abe Lebewohl. "My wife was shopping there recently, and it was packed. All of a sudden, she's asked to leave. Ten minutes later, she's invited back. One minute it's a grocery store, the next minute it's a *shul.*"

During one crowded prayer time, a worshipper standing next to the refrigerated cabinet casually opened it and aligned the packages of J. & J. country-sweet butter. Another absentmindedly toyed with a coffee cake, while a third eyed Smith's bubble gum and then prodded a jar of

Rokeach Redi-Jelled *gefilte* fish. When a woman tried the door and found it locked, one worshipper raised his eyes from his prayer book only long enough to signal her to be patient.

As business resumed, Mr. Bistritzky explained that he had invented this combination of free enterprise and rigid devotion seven years earlier, when his father died. Needing a place to say *kaddish*, the prayer for the dead, and having neighbors eager to say *mincha*, he invited them over. A quorum of ten—a *minyan*—is required for public worship, and getting one was no trick at all in this stretch of the Lower East Side.

At about four o'clock, as though habits needed reminders, Mr. Bistritzky telephones his friends to tell them the time. One call goes to the G. & M. kosher takeout shop ("Free Chicken Soup with Every Roast Chicken"). Michael Fleischer answers. "All Bistritzky says is 'Mincha,' and since I know who's calling around four, I usually answer 'Thank you' before he has a chance to say 'Mincha.'"

Around the corner on Hester Street, at the H. & M. Skullcap Manufacturing Company, where business is booming, Mr. Bistritzky's call puts a daily crimp in production. With bar mitzvahs mobilizing, weddings marching, and special yarmulkes demanded for these occasions, every minute is precious. But when the call comes, Meilech Torn and Hersh Reinman, partners and brothers-in-law, stop the assembly line, clap hats over their yarmulkes, and run out of the store, trailed by their employees.

"It can rain, it can snow, it can lightning—there's *mincha* at Bistritzky's," said Mr. Torn. "He's a man with a soul. Nobody else would do it—close a store when he has twenty customers. If it weren't for him, a lot of Jews wouldn't be praying. So when he calls we answer."

Since not even the telephone is perfect, Mr. Bistritzky

often goes to his door and shouts a toll-free "Mincha! Mincha!" at the switching hour.

An imposing man in his fifties, with a twenty-year beard, he sometimes leads the prayers himself. During the busy season a young man he knows who chants even faster is encouraged to take over, and finishes in less than the usual time.

"To close the store and go to a *shul* and then try to get a *minyan*—and maybe fail—would take too long," Mr. Bistritzky said. "Customers usually understand when they see us praying, but some people say, 'Always I come when you're praying.'"

Mr. Bistritzky has ten children and nine grandchildren, eleven of them males. He feels that his *minyan* problems may solve themselves once all the males are of age to favor his grocery with their prayers.

This Is the Way God Has Created It

Barely three months had passed since Yoineh Meir had become a slaughterer, but the time seemed to stretch endlessly. He felt as though he were immersed in blood and lymph. His ears were beset by the squawking of hens, the crowing of roosters, the gobbling of geese, the lowing of oxen, the mooing and bleating of calves and goats; wings fluttered, claws tapped on the floor. The bodies refused to know any justification or excuse—every body resisted in its own fashion, tried to escape, and seemed to argue with the Creator to its last breath.

From *The Slaughterer*, by Isaac Bashevis Singer

When he was about three years old, in Poland, Isaac Bashevis Singer came running home one day and told his mother, in childhood Yiddish: "Man hits pig and pig is crying."

"I was crying, too," he recalled. "I had pity on the *chazer*, the pig. I felt even guilty when I walked on the street and stepped on a worm. I said to myself, 'I walk on

71

him and he has no choice.' From my childhood I saw that might is right in nature, and it bothered me terribly. I saw the slaughterer standing there with a knife and killing a chicken, and I said there is no evidence whatsoever that we are more important than a chicken. It is just that the slaughterer has the knife—he can kill this chicken, and the chicken can never appeal to anybody. It is legal, it is kosher, it is everything."

Mr. Singer was to become celebrated—even win the Nobel Prize for Literature—when his Yiddish stories were translated and published in English. As he observed and described life, might was everywhere triumphant: "At school the stronger boys hit the weaker, majorities oppressed minorities, strong countries ruled small ones. They said they will do away with 'might is right' in Soviet Russia, and then came a Stalin and he had so much might and he was so right, almost as much as Hitler."

"This is the way God has created it," Mr. Singer explained to himself. "There is nothing we can do about it. He wants it this way."

"But I don't have to praise the Almighty for this," he said. "I don't have to say, 'You are right.' He *may* be right. He may know that the man of today will be the beetle of tomorrow, and the beetle a man. But since I don't have the information, I don't have to say thank you. I admire God's wisdom, which everybody can see, but I don't praise Him for His mercy, because His mercy I cannot see. It's not my duty to praise a mercy which I don't understand, which in my eyes looks like cruelty.

"The very fact that He is Almighty already expressed the idea that might is right. I sometimes have a feeling that it would have been better if He wouldn't have been so almighty, if there would have been some competition, and if somebody could have told Him that it's not enough to be mighty and clever; you also must explain to your victims why they suffer, not just let them do all the guesswork.

"It is true that the Talmud says that one should thank God for the evil things just as much as we thank Him for the good things. But I feel we don't have to be so humble. The Bible and the Talmud were all man-made, and I don't have to agree a hundred percent, nor does anybody else. What I like there I take, and what I don't like I don't take."

Making up his own mind, in Warsaw before World War II, Mr. Singer became a vegetarian one morning, and in the evening he changed his mind. After emigrating to America, he tried repeatedly to follow principle instead of appetite, each time succumbing to desire and suffering the pangs of guilt.

One day about fifteen years ago, Mr. Singer's pet parakeet, who was not kept in a cage, fell into a vase and drowned. "I imagined the struggle which this poor animal had," he said, "because a parakeet is light—he doesn't drown so quickly. It took him perhaps hours. When I thought about this, I said to myself, 'What are you waiting for? If the death of this little animal can hurt you so much, what about the larger animals?'"

Since then he has shunned meat and fish. Some years ago a woman wanted him to sign a petition in favor of "humane" slaughter. "I don't believe in humane slaughter," he told her. "Once it's slaughter, it's not humane."

Though he has written about slaughterers who suffer terrible nightmares, he does not consider them more guilty than those who eat meat. "I've seen slaughterers who in private life were very charitable and good-natured people," he said. "Our grandmothers used to cut up a fish for the Shabbas. They were not cruel people. They were brought up on this. They never questioned. In my eyes a slaughterer is not a criminal, but neither is he a great hero."

When Mr. Singer lectures on literature, there are often dinners in his honor; hosts who know that he is a vegetarian often prepare a vegetarian meal for everyone. "So, in a very small way, I do a favor for the chickens," Mr. Singer said. "If I will ever get a monument, chickens will do it for me. But actually I haven't done enough for them. I could make propaganda, but I'm not a propagandist by nature. Since I really don't know the Almighty's purposes and the way He conducts the world, there's no sense throwing my convictions on others. I never feel that I am in any way better than the man who eats meat. Other people do other good things which I don't do. They give charity, they help people, they fight for causes."

His wife, who contributes to organizations that care for animals, is not a vegetarian: "She said to me, 'Why do you do it? You may get sick, God forbid!' But since she saw that nothing happens to me she made peace with it. I don't think it has done me any damage. I enjoy my food. And how I enjoy my food! I enjoy the blintz to the last bite. When I come into a restaurant and someone is eating boiled beef with horseradish, the desire is there, but I wouldn't eat meat for any money in the world."

• • •

As a child in Latvia, Pinchas M. Teitz used to visit the market and see people beating animals. "I couldn't stand it," he said. "The Bible says that cruelty to animals is forbidden, and yet it says that you may slaughter an animal and use its flesh. Se we have to make sure there's no pain to the animal. The knife must be sharp; it should have no indentation. With one swift stroke that cuts through the esophagus, carotid and veins, stopping the blood to the brain, the animal is senseless. This is done by a man who has studied, a pious man who realizes that he cannot be guilty of causing pain."

Rabbi Teitz moved to this country in 1936. He heads an Orthodox congregation in Elizabeth, New Jersey, and supervises a slaughterhouse where each week about six thousand animals are killed. There are twenty-two *shochtim*, men who slaughter according to religious law. "They do not consider it killing as such," the rabbi said. "They're doing a service to the community—providing meat to sustain lives."

"Our sense of morality is not for society to decide," he said. "Society may change. In order to have eternal, unchangeable principles, we must refer to our greatest authority, which is the Bible. The Bible says you can eat meat, so it is not a question of 'might makes right.'"

Adam was given dominion over the fish of the sea and the fowl of the air and over everything that moved upon the earth, the rabbi said, adding: "Man was appointed to serve God, and animals to serve man. When a man eats meat, he elevates the animal into a higher form of life, giving strength to the human spirit.

"I do not criticize a vegetarian if he's sincere," the rabbi said. "I test him not in his eating but in his behavior toward others. If he's a person of truth, justice, mercy, charity, I can understand. But if he shows mercy to animals and disregards human beings, then I don't believe it's mercy he shows the animal. He's trying to make up for the fact that he is not human to human beings. He's a *tzaddik*—a righteous man—when it comes to animals, but he's wicked the rest of the time."

The rabbi opened the Book of Proverbs and read aloud: "A righteous man regardeth the life of his beast, but the tender mercies of the wicked are cruel." "Start with people," he said. "When you pass the examination and you know your mind is pure, *then* become a vegetarian. Until then you're not a vegetarian—it's not a principle; it's just another diet."

Rabbi Teitz said that he had met many who called themselves vegetarians, but only one he considered sincere: "One in my whole life, and he was a saintly man. But with the others—with hypocrites—you can't do anything. So better stay away from them. Health is not contagious. Disease is contagious."

"There's a Yiddish saying," the rabbi said: " 'God you *cannot* fool, your fellow man you *dare* not fool, and if you fool yourself, you *are* a fool.' "

Deli

Martin Schloss was deep in coleslaw when he looked up and saw Abe Lebewohl, owner of the Second Avenue Delicatessen. Mr. Schloss lives on the West Side, and before he can get to the Second Avenue he must trek across blighted, deli-less wastes. "When are you going to open a West Side branch?" he asked.

Mr. Lebewohl sighed and looked heavenward, as though only enemies would wish him such blessings. "If I opened all the places people wanted me to," he said, "I'd have more branches than A&P, if I could keep them open."

Reinforcements of coleslaw arrived just in time to join the mushroom and barley soup, and Mr. Schloss's neighbor leaned across her table and delicately, smiling indulgently, took a spoonful from Mrs. Schloss's bowl.

On a Saturday night, to say nothing of the other six nights into which the food is compressed, an Emily Post might raise an eyebrow, but if she stayed around long enough she'd raise a spoon as well.

"When was the last time you made mushroom barley soup like this?" Mr. Schloss asked his wife.

"I always make mushroom barley soup," she replied, then added: "All right, not like this."

"The hunger pains are coming two minutes apart," exulted Eva Meadows, as her spoon flailed rhythmically.

A steady client once suggested that Mr. Lebewohl copy the airlines and have oxygen masks drop automatically to keep clients going. Food here is so popular that there are often people outside waiting for admission. This upsets Mr. Lebewohl, so he treats them to canapés of chopped liver, tuna, and chopped eggs with mushrooms and *shmaltz*. Touched by the suffering of devotees waiting in cold or rain, he used to hire a double-decker bus for shelter at curbside. But people complained that they'd already been on a bus to get to the deli.

"We lived on Second Avenue when it was the Jewish Broadway," Amy Yefroikin said. "I know more people in the cemetery than in New York City. Actually, you can die if you order a meal here at the Second Avenue Delicatessen. What they consider an appetizer is a portion—and such a portion!"

Mrs. Yefroikin's friend Zalman J. Lichtenstein is faithful to matzoh ball soup and chicken fricassee. "I was all over the world, she was all over the world, and you can't get chicken fricassee like this anyplace else," he said. "And at the end of the meal I must have a glass of tea. I will never take a cup of tea. Where else can you get a glass of tea?"

"At the Russian Tea Room," said Mrs. Yefroikin.

"It isn't even Russian anymore," he rejoined.

"Every year we have a luncheon for retired members of the International Ladies Garment Workers Union," he went on, "and last October we had a thousand delegates at the Americana. If there had been enough room at the Second Avenue Delicatessen we would have brought them here. This is the Last Mohican of Jewish culinary art."

Peter Cippoletti, who is not Jewish but who speaks richly idiomatic Yiddish, is another regular here. He learned Yiddish as a grocer's delivery boy, before World War II, and keeps linguistically trim and physically full blown with weekly visits to the Second Avenue. Though Mr. Cippoletti has been eating here for more than ten years, Mr. Lebewohl remains astonished at his client's mastery of Jewish oral traditions.

When Mr. Lebewohl, who was born in Poland, came to this country, he got a job as a delicatessen counterman, and in 1954 he and the manager opened a place of their own. "He found a *landsman* who went broke as a furrier—we needed a waiter anyway, so we were three partners," Mr. Lebewohl said. "Business was bad. We drew $50 a week, and the dishwasher got $40, although we worked three times as hard. Everyone wanted out, and there was nobody to pay us out."

The furrier finally got out and went to Arizona to join his children. Mr. Lebewohl broke both legs and went home to find himself suddenly rich, drawing $110 insurance a week.

When he returned to the delicatessen, it was a fight to the finish between the two partners: who would be allowed to leave first? Finally Mr. Lebewohl got the money to pay off his partner, then paid off his suppliers and began living on earnings instead of credit.

When the local Yiddish theater shut down, Mr. Lebewohl thought the end was nigh and threw caution about antitrust laws to the winds. "I ran over to Ratner's [a nearby Jewish dairy restaurant] and told Mr. Harmatz we had to do something," he said. "Mr. Harmatz was the type—'Let's wait and see'—he didn't want to do anything."

Mr. Lebewohl got the mad idea of modernizing and expanding, a notion that horrified his friends. He recalled his attorney saying, "Abe, in this neighborhood you're going to invest?"

The new place—still fully kosher—prospered as never before. In 1974, to celebrate twenty years of making money, Mr. Lebewohl went all out to lose some. For one day he cut prices to what they had been when he first opened for business. To make sure the word got out, he took newspaper ads. To make sure the customers got in, he hired a Pinkerton man to maintain order. The customers made it without any trouble and gorged on corned beef sandwiches for 50 cents, matzoh ball soup for 30 cents, coffee for a nickel. But the Pinkerton man, descendant of a long line of detectives, could not find the delicatessen. By the time he arrived, concealing his chagrin behind set jaw and flinty eye, a crowd had filled the delicatessen, and the overflow stood in a line down Second Avenue.

"I figure for every dollar that comes in, $1.10 goes out," said Mr. Lebewohl, struggling with a smile.

The first customer was Rabbi Stephen Lerner of nearby Tifereth Israel—Town and Village Synagogue. "Do you really want people to know about this?" he asked Mr. Lebewohl. "The more people who come, the more you lose."

Rabbi Lerner ordered a pastrami sandwich and potato salad (50 cents plus 20 cents), and then a corned beef sandwich with potato salad. Tea came to a nickel. "The Talmud says you have to have a just price," said the rabbi. "This price is too low to be just."

As the rabbi finished his second sandwich, the Messengers—a two-piece Hasidic combo—arrived. "I have no room for the Messengers," Mr. Lebewohl cried.

"Suspend them from the ceiling, like a go-go act," the rabbi suggested.

"The prices are too high," said Harry Golden, corned beef in cheek. "Who ever heard of 50 cents for a corned beef sandwich!"

"I had a roast beef sandwich," said Harold Cooper. "It didn't taste like it was twenty years old."

When Mr. Lebewohl first announced that he was going to cut prices for his anniversary, regular customers called to say they would avoid the crush. But Lee Romm, one of the veteran faithful, couldn't bear the sacrifice. "The delicatessen's not only good today," she said, "it's good all the time."

Helping out were Mr. Lebewohl's wife, Eleanore, as receptionist; his father, Efraim, at the cash register; his brother Jack as—well, as Jack-of-all-trades; and Jack's wife, Terry. But service was slightly slower than usual, what with waiters doing little dance steps as they went to and from the counter.

Mrs. Lillian Berg waited patiently. "I'm not hungry, but I couldn't resist a bargain," she said, as split pea soup (20 cents) arrived, followed by roast beef sandwich (50 cents). "I ate before, and I just wanted to come in and have a nosh."

When there was a meat shortage several years ago, exorbitant payments to suppliers kept the kitchen going. "My chef was standing with cabbage leaves, and he didn't have any meat," Mr. Lebewohl recalled. "What could I do? Where I am, I'm not where people are. I have to bring people here."

To minimize desecration from wayward trips of chicken *shmaltz,* menus are printed each day and served fresh daily. Except during weekends, clients are invited to order half-sandwiches if the worst happens and they are hungry at the end of a meal. But Mr. Lebewohl also offers a full-size "open sandwich medley"—corned beef, tongue, roast beef, turkey, pastrami, chopped liver, salami, eggs and mushrooms, and potato salad—serving four hungry souls or three famished ones.

Phyllis Brienza, a waitress who works here weekends, had trouble at first pronouncing *"kasha varnitchkes"* (buckwheat groats with twists of pasta). "I went home and practiced, but the words stuck to the roof of my mouth," she said.

Tom Lyttle, a veteran waiter with a passion for opera, warbles his orders faultlessly to the countermen. "How did you like the opera?" he asked one client whom he had seen at the Metropolitan days earlier.

"I knew you from somewhere, and I didn't remember from where," she apologized.

"If I'd been carrying a corned beef sandwich you would have recognized me," he said, gently reproachful.

As she waited at the counter, Florence Eidinger spoke of her own abiding faith: "Last week we ordered a great big turkey for my mother-in-law's eighty-fifth birthday, and we told Abe we wanted it hot at two o'clock. We got a hot turkey at two o'clock—it wasn't a cold turkey at two-thirty."

"Abe's *kishkes* are out of this world," her husband said.

"My favorite food is food," Mr. Lebewohl said, "but I don't enjoy eating a meal here in the store. I feel guilty that I should be eating instead of working. But I enjoy eating out in a restaurant, especially if things go wrong. Then I see other people have problems too."

Deli Waiters

Jewish waiters, who are used to giving the orders, turned polite and deferred to astonished customers on July 4th. It was Independence Day, and the emancipated Jewish waiter marked the occasion in the most astonishing way, with a revolutionary change of face.

It has been said that Israel won the Six-Day War by putting guns into the hands of Jewish waiters. But on July 4th they laid down their arms. Snarls were out; smiles were in. Waiters grown irascible on endless servings of chopped liver and chicken soup beamed with good nature, and from every pore oozed the sour cream of human kindness.

"It's the changing of the guard at Buckingham Palace," said Irving Goldberg as he waited solicitously on customers at the Sixth Avenue Delicatessen. "It's a holiday. We're a frisky, devil-may-care bunch today."

In the holiday stillness, the rage to advance, gobble, and retreat suddenly became a gentle amble toward dyspepsia. For the first time in months, waiters managed moments for a smile as they surveyed the scenes of former triumphs and wondered where they would win their next victory.

A man preparing outgoing orders looked up from the Moshe Dayan ("Jewish hero") sandwich he was fortifying, gazed out at the strangely pacific spectacle, and declared: "The waiters used to be nervous and jerky. They're not nervous anymore. Two English muffins!"

At the Stage Delicatessen, a waiter tried earnestly to explain the startling change. "It's Independence Day," he said, "and who could be more independent than the Jewish waiter? Since we have 364 days of independence, we're allowing ourselves one day to be different."

But it was difficult. When a client asked a waiter at the Stage why he wasn't wearing a name badge, he replied: "Why should I wear my name? Everybody calls me names, anyway."

As hours went by without name-calling, a new light of hope came into his eye, although an occasional shadowy reflex betrayed the rest of the year. When one customer looked up from the menu to ask if the melon was fresh, the waiter came to himself and snapped, "What's the matter with the melon? You haven't had it yet. It's as fresh as me, and I'm damned fresh."

But then he selected a specially luscious melon, and his face almost creaked as he delivered himself of melon and smile.

A policeman who walked into the Stage Delicatessen looked incredulously about him at the strangely happy multitude, and the manager said playfully, "You're under arrest."

"All right," said the man in blue, "as long as you keep me in here."

Even as an employee telephoned to ask why forty-two loaves of rye-bread-without-labels had not arrived in time, the manager looked unperturbed, as though there would be a valid excuse.

At the Carnegie Delicatessen, a waiter was singing as customers arrived. When two moved from the table to which he had assigned them, he muttered to himself: "You'll sit where I put you." But then he remembered the day, smiled indulgently, and sang an octave higher.

For long-suffering victims, it was a glorious interlude. They could change their minds without harassment, order small without derision, eat slowly without concern. When a customer asked one waiter what had wrought this extraordinary change, the waiter replied: "Maybe the firecrackers hit us."

He added quickly: "We could change very fast."

Brochos Bee

SPELLING BEES everybody knows about, from *a* to *ʒ*. But only a minority knows about blessing bees—competitions to recall appropriate blessings, from man to God.

When the National Society for Hebrew Day Schools held its fifth annual *Brochos* (Blessings) Bee at its headquarters in Manhattan, winners from scores of schools competed in the finals. Since the road to piety is paved with good retentions, these children had swotted long hours to remember the fine differences.

One blessing applies to moderate quantities of pastry, another to gorging. Over fruit that grows on trees, the appropriate formula is "Who created the fruit of the tree"; over produce grown in or close to the ground, the blessing becomes "Who created the fruit of the earth." An ice cream cone demands a blessing for the cone, another for the ice cream.

There are blessings for a glimpse of the ocean, of trees in spring, of the new moon, or of a rainbow. On seeing a strange being, one thanks God for varying the forms of His creatures. On seeing an emperor, one must offer a blessing. Even if the clothes have no emperor, a blessing is demanded as appropriate to his glory.

Care must be taken not to utter a blessing in vain, God forbid, though there is a blessing appropriate to a vain blessing, namely: "Blessed be the name of His glorious kingdom forever and ever."

Upon hearing a benediction, one says, "Blessed be He and blessed be His name," and also "Amen." The A must not be rushed, nor the n dropped; "Amen" demands deliberate speed, lest one be guilty of what is known as "an orphaned Amen."

Right up until the last Amen, parents were barred. As one rabbi closed the door in the face of parents trying to squeeze into the room where junior girls would be tested, he pleaded: "All right, so they'll lose. It's all that could happen!"

Fast and curious the questions came: What is the blessing appropriate to almonds, American cheese, angel food cake, apples...? Down went contestants—on buckwheat, chives, éclair, eggplant, grits, *kasha*, parsley. Finally, Reana Bookson, age six, stumbled on rhubarb, leaving Elaine Witty, eight, a triumphant winner.

So stubbornly expert were the senior girls that Rabbi Abraham Fishelis was driven to extremes: "What happens if you hear good news that will eventually become bad news?" Finally, Beverly Oppenheimer admitted she did not know what to say on receiving new dishes, while Lisa Ann Clare recited flawlessly in Hebrew—"Who is good and who does good to others."

Among the intermediate boys, the rabbi's questions produced counter-questions. Applesauce—"Homemade or store-bought?" Borsht—"With potatoes?"

Pizza's blessing depended on the number of slices. Noted

the society's Rabbi Bernard Goldenberg: "Comes America, comes a cosmopolitan town like New York, and pizza becomes an issue. You can have one slice of pizza, as a snack, which takes one kind of blessing. But what if you decide to have two slices or three? Then it's not a fast-food approach. I'm sitting down. I'm making a meal. It's a different blessing."

An especially learned rabbi was "Supreme Court," and he faced staggering problems. "They're still arguing over the *knaydlach* [matzoh balls]," Rabbi Goldenberg said happily.

There was naturally a blessing appropriate for the winners, and of course one equally fitting for the losers: "Blessed art Thou, O Lord our God, King of the Universe, the true Judge."

Soup

AT THE ISRAELI GOVERNMENT'S Food Show in Manhattan, there are enough soups on display to float the *Queen Miriam:* mushroom barley, green pea, borsht, potato, vegetable, onion, celery, asparagus, tomato, even a Hebrew Alef-Bet soup in which the letters float from right to left. But if it's maybe a chicken soup you're looking for, you should be patient.

Shalom's assortment includes a cube which "tastes like homemade consommé." "A chickeny taste," explains Stanley Bauman, the importer's national sales manager. All right—chickeny. But chicken it's not.

Osem's cup runneth over with things to put into its soups, such as mini *mandelen* (small croutons) and maxi *mandelen* (not so small croutons). But chicken? Not even to save a life.

The problem is that the U.S. Department of Agriculture will not allow the import of Israeli chicken products until further inspection can be arranged.

Enter Telma soups, advertising Israeli chicken soup.

How does chicken get into this broth? The question is no sooner put than Isaac Levine rushes in. "What's the question?" he asks.

"Where's the chicken?"

"That's a good question," replies Mr. Levine, and hurriedly consults colleagues. The secret comes out. The chickens are American. Parts of them are shipped to Israel to provide chicken to put into the soup which is then shipped back to America to be sold as chicken soup.

And if you want a little sweetness at the end of the meal, Henry Gottlieb of Brooklyn's Jaret International is distributor for The Nazareth Candy Co. Ltd., of Nazareth. At the food show he offers kosher Santa Clauses. "Everything that comes out of the factory is kosher, so the Santa Clauses are kosher; but if you publicize that they're kosher, gentiles won't buy," says Mr. Gottlieb. "Jewish people won't buy them kosher or not kosher."

He provides Santas in various sizes. The six-pack giant Santas (including three bells) retail for two dollars, and small milk chocolate Santas for a dime each. He also has a line in kosher Easter eggs.

Potato
Pie in the Sky

EACH MAN DREAMS of his own kind of glory. One man wants to be president; another would like to be rich. Elias Gabay dreamed of making the perfect *knish*, and by the time he died—age eighty-two—he had made a great thing out of *knishes*.

Gabay called himself the "King of Potato Pies," and his *knishes* were heavy with mashed potatoes, tingling with spices, smoothly browned, so appetizing that you wanted another when one was more than enough. The company he started is the world's largest *knish*-maker, and its Brooklyn factory sends *knishes* fresh or frozen round the nation.

Gabay's origins were humble. He was born in the country that is now Yugoslavia, and he became a shoemaker—or, as befits a memory leavened with age—a "shoe stylist." "The price was so high he would make shoes only for royalty," said his lawyer and old friend Joseph Levine.

When Gabay married, it was in a Yugoslav town named Nish (as in *knish*), and in 1919 he and his wife emigrated to America. They arrived with 35 cents.

He worked in shoe factories, spent months out of work;

then, in 1926, the Gabays went into the restaurant business, in a basement on Forsythe Street on New York's Lower East Side. In this Forsythe saga, wife Bella did the cooking. She made dough so thin that when you blew on it, it flew away. A customer asked if she could make blintzes with potatoes in them instead of cheese, and she began producing *knishes.* Her husband went out with a pushcart to sell them, and he acquired clients right down the length of Delancey Street.

One day a delicatessen in Brooklyn called with a huge order. "Brooklyn?" Gabay said. "What country is that?"

When he discovered that Brooklyn was across the bridge, he bought a little truck and, using the only free time he had—in the middle of the night—learned to drive.

In 1928 the Gabay family moved to Brooklyn, almost under the shadow of the Williamsburg bridge. The new home was a shack, but soon more and more *knishes* were coming out of the hot oil. Since the name Gabay lends itself to different pronunciations, the *knish* company began calling itself Gabila (rhymes with *megilla*).

In his moves, Gabay had picked up large chunks of Spanish, Ladino, Serbo-Croatian, Greek, Russian, Bulgarian, Rumanian, Polish, Italian, French, Yiddish and Hebrew. His friends pressed him to tape-record the story of his life—in any language but English, they suggested, so that people would understand him.

When Gabay applied for United States citizenship, he didn't know how to read or write English—he was that busy with *knishes.* Gabay handed the judge a card identifying himself as monarch of *knish*-makers. "I have five children and I'm a king already," he pointed out. "I'll make a good citizen."

"I guess you will," the judge said, and approved the application.

"Gabay always had to do things in a special way," his first lawyer, Nathan M. Padgug, recalled. "When he bought a car, it had to be different. His horn couldn't be like other people's horns. Gabay's horn had to say, 'Hoo HOO! Hoo HOO!'"

After a hard day of producing and selling and delivering, Gabay would take Bella out, and night after night they won prizes—not for *knishes,* but for dancing. "Until he was about eighty," said Levine, "he was one of the finest ballroom dancers in the country."

"A regular Beau Brummel," added Levine's partner, Isadore Kupfer.

"He was equal to Adolphe Menjou," said Levine. "Debonair even when he didn't have a nickel. When Adolphe Menjou wore a derby and spats and carried a cane, that was him. Once he used his cane to stop a cattle stampede on the Williamsburg bridge."

As business grew, Gabay dreamed of a machine that would produce *knishes* untouched by human hands, and he worked to realize his dream.

In the modernized factory, molds and pipes and transmission belts jostle for space and glory. An intricate complex of potato washer and peeler and sorter leads to steamer and masher and drainpipes. Brushes are fitted into place like gentle hands, flicking excess flour from *knishes* moving along the line. A stainless steel horizontal hand moves rhythmically up and down, patting each *knish* as it passes.

"Everything is automatic," said Levine, glancing past white-gloved workers gently helping the *knishes* on their way. His eye detected a worker shoveling potato mix with a shovel. "You see," he said, snatching a moral from the jaws of disillusion, "even a stainless steel shovel."

"It comes out like raindrops—look at the beauty," he said reverently as the *knishes* fell gently out of the boiling cottonseed oil. "Take this," he said to a visitor, "slice it, put some delicatessen—salami—in it, and you have the finest dish in the world."

The Gabays zealously guard the secrets of this automated equipment. Levine, who speaks of Gabila in the assimilative "we," said: "We never got a patent, because if we got a patent we'd have to disclose."

Four of the original Gabays' five children now run the company; the fifth lives in Florida. Explained Levine: "Isaac is sort of equipment, Hymel is production, Clara and Sophie are office and bookkeeping."

A grandson, Elliot Gabay, is learning the business. "It would be a pity to let it die," he said.

"Today we ship our *knishes* everywhere," said Isaac Gabay. "In Dad's day, if a small man tried to get into Times Square, he couldn't do it. Today we have all of Times Square, we have Shea Stadium, the Big A, all the beaches, schools and colleges. There are even stainless Gabila carts outside the fanciest department stores."

"We have two words—service and quality," noted Levine. "What do they say about the mail carriers? 'Neither rain nor snow'? Well, when it rains we go on working, and when it snows we stay at the machines. If the employees can't get to work, we go out to get them. Nothing keeps *knishes* from their appointed place."

Visit to a
Matzoh Factory

"WHO CAN TELL me the reason for the holes in the matzohs?" asked Rabbi Joseph Braver.

"So it can't like puff up," replied one boy.

The rabbi beamed. "And what are we not allowed to eat during Passover?" he pursued.

"Leavened bread," another boy answered.

The visit to the Manischewitz matzoh factory in Jersey City was just beginning, and the pupils from the Beth Sholom Hebrew School of Union, New Jersey, stirred impatiently in their chairs. They were taking a day off from school for a tour of the factory, and here was their rabbi acting just like a rabbi.

Finally, he turned them over to the factory manager, Arthur Feuer, and the assistant manager, Joseph Botwinick. The children hurried out of the factory's synagogue and clambered up the stairs to see wheat being mixed with water and baked.

The wheat used for matzoh must be free of moisture, bleaches and additives. To ensure fidelity to the instructions of Bible and Talmud, rabbis stay on the job twenty-four hours, and even sleep at the mill. When the wheat is mixed with water and baked, the duty-rabbis stand by again, making sure the mix stands no longer than eighteen minutes—to avoid fermentation before it goes into the oven.

Chaim Karlinsky, the head rabbi at the factory, sees to it also that the *chalah*—a bit of dough—is removed from each mix. "According to law," he explains, "the *chalah* should be given to a Cohen. Today we don't know if everyone who's called Cohen is a real Cohen, so we burn the *chalah.*"

"I smell coconut macaroons," said Mr. Feuer.

"Even the rabbi can smell what's cooking," said Rabbi Karlinsky, urging visitors to take a Certificate of Kashrut certifying that factory products are "Kosher... for Passover... beyond a shadow of a doubt."

To make the shadow even smaller, three other rabbis had signed the document, adding "With the help of G-d; February 18, 1969."

Rabbi Karlinsky explained the omission of a letter by saying: "The Bible says not to take God's name in vain. Sometimes with paper you're throwing it away and it lies on the floor, and that would be taking God's name in vain. To express His name you're allowed, but not to throw away."

After touring the production line, the visitors went to the dining room to sample production.

Mrs. Lucy Kirshenbaum, a teacher, tried to shepherd the children into some order, and Mr. Botwinick said to her: "Sit down—don't be a typical Jewish mother. Leave the kids alone."

She turned away to give another teacher her recipe for fried matzoh.

"Can you make matzohs that look like bread?" a child asked.

"Wash your mouth out with kosher soap," replied Mr. Botwinick, barely interrupting his own account of the ideal matzoh ball. "I would never eat a matzoh ball unless it weighs a ton," he said.

"Can you use *shmaltz* to make matzoh balls?" asked a mother.

"Oil," he said.

"My grandmother used *shmaltz,*" she insisted.

"You want to use *shmaltz,*" he said, "use *shmaltz.*"

When the children filed out, each received a paper bag filled with Manischewitz specials. Suddenly a worker rushed up to report an emergency.

"The *farfel* is backed up all the way to the penthouse," he shouted.

Farfel is a Jewish vermicelli, and everybody knows what a penthouse is—except at the matzoh factory. There it's a bulge in the roof where the pipes stick out.

"You see," said Mr. Feuer proudly and calmly, "we always have an emergency."

Matzoh Brei

OF COURSE the mayor of New York City was invited to the Fourth Matzoh *Brei* Convention, but he was committed to austerity, so he made do with a telegram: "I wish you continued success in your endeavors to further ideas that we all affirm."

Matzoh *brei* is more than an idea, and it's not enough to affirm it. It's a delicacy, and anyone with a palate should taste it: crumbled matzoh soaked in an egg batter, then fried and served delicious and hot.

The Fourth Matzoh *Brei* Convention steered clear of fancy hotels and came to order at Farm Food Restaurant, 142 West 49th Street. Forty fully committed delegates attended, bearing the only credentials necessary: six dollars to pay for the meal.

Notice of each year's convention spreads by word of open mouth—the Matzoh Party has no dues, no obligations, no membership lists. Said Paul Feingold, a delegate from Riverdale: "Some organizations meet every week. They have a procedure; they have a purpose. By the time they're finished meeting, everybody's depressed. With us there's no purpose, and nobody ever gets depressed. What happens to our stomachs is another matter. The entire constitution of this organization is written in chicken fat. We haven't got any amendments because we haven't got enough chicken fat."

Experts on the constitution are still arguing about which came first, the chicken fat or the egg, but the matzoh's development is clear. It goes back to the Biblical exodus from Egypt, when housewives rushing to escape took unleavened dough with them, which the desert sun then baked. Matzoh *brei* is therefore traditional during the spring Passover holiday commemorating the exodus.

"It's like pumpkin pie which sells marvelously at Thanksgiving, and the day after you couldn't give one away," said Harold Swersky, owner of Farm Food. "So why is the convention held in November? It's to perpetuate the memory.

"I myself eat matzoh *brei* on the first day of Passover, on the middle day, and finally on the last day, to carry me through the year. Passover has eight days, and there's a subtle intelligence involved in the cooking—because it takes six days to learn to make them and the last two days they're great."

Farm Food's way is to crumble matzoh dry into a batter of eggs, milk, salt and a little pepper. "And should I tell you the secret?" Mr. Swersky asked. "A little cinnamon sugar. Whether or not they like it, it goes into the batter."

He hurried to the kitchen to inspect preparations. Heretically, his cooks had made the matzoh *brei* in advance. Mr. Swersky looked at the stacks mournfully, struggling with his emotions. "Max," he said to the nearest cook, "you made them just as usual—too well done."

As he emerged from the kitchen, he bumped into Jackie

Gibson, a delegate from Rockland County. "I got up off my deathbed," she said. "I'm tired, I'm aching, but I made it."

"Wait till she eats it," muttered Mr. Feingold. "Matzoh *brei* will cement us all together—if we eat enough of it."

"It was wished on the Jews by all the anti-Semites in history," he added, not meaning a word of all that. "It's one of the double crosses we have to bear as Jews."

At the microphone, Lee Evers, representing Manhattan Conservatives, banged a spoon to get attention as a hungry delegate impatiently cried "Impeach him!" Unperturbed, Mr. Evers introduced his wife the chairlady.

"We are gathered here tonight to honor the matzoh *brei*," she began. "We find it very sad that in our homes and the homes of our friends the matzoh *brei* is becoming a memory and not even a memory. This convention keeps the taste of it alive."

"For a whole year," Mr. Feingold called out.

When the delegates had cleared their palates with fruit salad, waiters and waitresses emerged from the kitchen in triumph, bearing matzoh *brei*. There was promptly a floor demonstration which the chairlady gaveled into a semblance of order.

At his table, Christopher Tabori sat bemused. "I'm of the Liberal denomination in matzoh *brei*," he said. "I'd never deign to say I prefer it this way or that way. Who am I to say I prefer it one way? I'm half-Jewish, and the most I can do when I stand up is pivot: my Jewish side is weighed down. Matzoh *brei* has changed my life—ever since high school, when I decided I didn't want to be euphoric, I wanted to be paralyzed."

Malcolm Varon was all kinetics, piling applesauce atop jam on sour cream resting in sugar which covered his matzoh *brei*. As soon as he had wolfed down the first serving, he called for seconds.

"There's always one in a crowd," said Mr. Feingold, and shouted, "I advise everybody to have seconds. I've just bought some Pepto-Bismol stock."

"Why don't you give an award for the man-of-the-year who ate two matzoh *breis?*" he suggested to fellow delegates. "That's the first time since Moses came down from the mountain."

When it was time for nominating speeches, nobody wanted to run for office. "The election is fixed, just like real elections," said retiring president William Gladstone, who keeps hoping somebody else will write the matzoh *brei* newsletters and give him more time to eat.

Eric Margenau was finally elected president by acclamation barely loud enough to drown his protests. Mr. Gladstone refused to let him off, and blithely continued to savor the Israeli matzoh used in Farm Food's matzoh *brei.*

With Gladstone you expect to find Israeli, and while the retiring president chewed away, his fellow delegates cheered his final hours in office with tributes and laments.

"Cassava melon, caviar and marinara sauce are all world-famous," said Mr. Tabori, "and matzoh *brei* is left to languish in the desert."

"The only thing I want is to leave you with an ethnic slogan," said Mr. Feingold, holding his fork aloft like a scepter. "'Don't quit till matzoh *brei* is as popular as pizza.'"

Food Show

"A BREAKTHROUGH!" cried chef Latzi Wittenberg at his stand on the Starlight Roof of the Waldorf-Astoria. "Mission Possible in the kosher-food business."

Visitors to the one-day show of the Institutional Kosher Food Manufacturers Association raved over Mr. Wittenberg's unusual delights—a Chicken Breast Wellington (with beef and chopped liver), a Royal Hawaiian Wellington (with sweetbreads and pineapple) and a Rothschild Wellington (with chopped beef and turkey).

Rothschild all right, but why Wellington? "There were some famous Jews in Britain," explained Mr. Wittenberg, "and I think Wellington would like to have his name associated with Jewish foods."

"My stomach is my laboratory," he said, "but thank God I also have a test kitchen and I have a person to convince—my wife Rachel."

She doled out samples while her husband mused: "Other manufacturers of kosher food have frozen chicken, boiled chicken, chicken with or without feathers. I didn't want to compete with chickens. I wanted to compete with my French and Italian colleagues."

Morton Silver, a chef at the Hebrew National Kosher Foods stand, explained the mysteries of his cuisine. Mr. Silver, who stands five feet three inches and weighs 225 pounds, said: "The secret of Jewish cooking is to like food. If you look at me you'll see what I mean. When I made the stuffed cabbage for Hebrew National, I made maybe 150 samples before I chose. We take samples of the food three times a day—for our own benefit. To me, after going through all the cooking, a plain piece of pumpernickel with a glass of milk is the best thing."

Almost everybody grown plump on Jewish cooking seemed to be there, noshing and wondering whether and how the show could help business.

Abe R. Goldin of the Zion Food Corporation tried to encourage the vogue for kosher Chinese food. "I think there are some Jews," he said, lowering his voice, "who like the roast pork of the Chinese. So our white-meat turkey roast with Chinese sauce tastes like pork."

Manischewitz was showing the kosher meals it supplies to passengers who travel Eastern or United. "Other airlines are breaking down the doors trying to get our kosher food," said Israel E. Werblowsky, who had no samples to give away. "It's an expensive thing," he explained. "An expensive thing you don't give away."

Irving Goldberg presided over relishes bottled by the Shaffer Grocery Corporation. "A lot of people are serving relish carts at catered functions," he noted. "A meal without relish is like a woman without earrings."

Jacob H. Tuchman, the caterer, nodded in agreement. "I just reminded myself we're having a bar mitzvah at the end of the month at the Plaza," he said. "I looked at the guest list, and I saw a man who, unless he gets pickles, the whole affair is not good."

From other producers there were *gefilte* fish, salami to end salamis, and *latkes* to begin heartburn with—a notion that upset Mr. Tuchman. "Jewish food doesn't give you heartburn," he insisted. "It's something within you that gives you heartburn."

Weight-Watchers
in Israel

MINNA AMSEL, an Israeli who was born in New York City, probably knows more people in Israel than anyone else. Not by face or by name, but by figure. She is the Jerusalem representative of Weight Watchers and runs an endless series of hortatory sessions in Hebrew for local people and in English for visiting students and tourists anxious not to interrupt Watching just because they happen to be in a Holy Land and could wait for a miracle to happen.

When Mrs. Amsel, who is in her forties and is decidedly—perhaps even excessively—svelte, walks or rides through Jerusalem, no obese person escapes her eye. She knows an extraordinary number of them to nod to, or to shake her head about. In this ancient city there are enormous vistas of excess poundage—by her estimate, one out of every three residents is overweight. Many of them are backsliders who were once with Weight Watchers, many others are with Weight Watchers, and the rest are prospects.

In a land where the language of love is "Eat! Eat!" Mrs.

Amsel says "Don't eat!" As she follows each adipose trail, she cannot help feeling unhappy that the offender has not yet got her message: "A person who's fat is a person who doesn't fit into society today. A thin person is a symbol of youth, vitality, beauty. A fat person represents age, sloth, a *shlep.*"

Israel is the quintessential land in which to watch out for weight. In the beginning was milk and honey, both fattening, and since then the diet has expanded to other calorific blessings: sweet fruit, heavy dough, cholesterol in a hundred guises. And then there is the volatile political situation.

"We're under constant tension here," explained Mrs. Amsel, "and one way to deal with tension is to eat. I know one woman who handled tension beautifully until her son went into the army. 'Minna,' she told me, 'until he's back, count me out.'"

The prophet who brought Weight Watchers out of the American wilderness into the Promised Land was Gina Dicker, who returned to her home on Long Island when she had accomplished her mission of mercy. She left behind a daughter, Bathseva Silverman. "My mother started Weight Watchers in Israel because she had a fat daughter here," explained Mrs. Silverman, who runs the head office in Tel Aviv. "I lost about eighty pounds, though I was skeptical to begin with. Like other Israelis, I'm a Doubting Thomas. Tell an Israeli not to eat something and he asks why."

Mrs. Amsel doubts not. Four years ago she herself lost fifty-five pounds. "I've kept myself down," she says, "and even gone downer." But she too has been weighed down by the Israeli proclivity for seeking explanations and reconfirmations. She recalls the story of the three men accidentally exposed to radiation poisoning. A doctor told them they were going to die, but each could be granted a final wish.

The Frenchman wanted a night out on the town with a beautiful woman, the Englishman wanted an audience with the Queen, and the Israeli wanted to see another doctor.

"People here want to know the why of it," complained Mrs. Amsel. "'So what will happen if I eat one little piece of cake?' They start to bargain with the scales, they bargain with me, they bargain with themselves. Sometimes I'm walking along the street and they're eating a piece of *falafel,* and they see me and choke over it. 'Oh, I didn't eat all day,' or the doctor said this or the doctor said that. A Weight Watcher in Israel will always say, 'Meet me near this bakery, or that restaurant.' Why never near a church or a synagogue?"

A surgeon once came to see Mrs. Amsel and briskly announced his cholesterol count, his blood sugar level, his weight, and how many pounds he wanted to lose. He explained that his hospital couldn't decide whether to cut a piece out of the operating table to make room for his stomach, or to cut a piece out of his stomach. At Weight Watchers he slimmed down—and ever since then he has refused to operate on overweight patients, except in emergencies, unless they try Weight Watchers first.

For reasons somewhat embarrassing to plumb, staff members at the Tel Aviv headquarters, having dropped from a peak of obesity, now appear stuck on a plateau of overweight. A couple of them are astonishingly rotund. Perhaps they are just waiting to catch their second wind before continuing the descent, or perhaps their doctors said this or that.

Since they are out of dieting practice, they preach. The staff sends out a four-page monthly newspaper bulging with good words and photographs, before and after, of successful dieters—police chiefs, housewives, government officials. The monthly also lists time and place of every Weight

Watchers meeting. About six thousand Israelis and visitors are enrolled in the mass effort. Many are doing marvelously; some are cheating like mad.

"People come after holidays," said Mrs. Silverman. "First they eat well, then they make good holiday resolutions and try to follow through. There's a big upsurge after Pesach and after Rosh haShanah. Wednesday groups are the smallest, because there's a full-length film on television that night."

For its Israeli clientele, Weight Watchers has devised recipes for slimming blintzes, lean cheesecake, and even *gefilte* fish made from carp that were themselves put on a diet before the ultimate sacrifice.

Under Mrs. Silverman's prodding, several kibbutzim have set up Weight Watchers tables in their dining halls. Givat Brenner, a large kibbutz, installed a Weight Watchers table for the twenty kibbutzniks who attend the Weight Watchers meetings at nearby Rehovot. Thirty kibbutzniks regularly turn up to nibble. The head office in Tel Aviv has magnanimously recommended that no one be turned away satisfied.

"People used to say we would have success with Anglo-Saxons and with West Europeans, but not with the Sephardic women, since Sephardic husbands like their women plump," Mrs. Silverman said. And when Mrs. Amsel went to a post office in Jerusalem to mail promotion brochures, the postal clerk (himself Sephardic) warned that sending them to Sephardic women was a waste of money—husbands wouldn't let their wives come.

"But they did come," Mrs. Amsel said. "In the beginning the Sephardic husbands thought it was ridiculous, but not in the end. Now we have a melting—a dissolving—pot, it's such a mixed group. We have women from Mea Sharim, the Orthodox section, next to women with miniskirts."

Everywhere in Israel there are women still unhappy about

their lot. After licking the knife with which she had been making cake icing, one woman dreamed she was in a mountain of icing and had to eat her way out. She woke in a cold sweat and came to see Mrs. Amsel. When a radio program on Kol Israel (Voice of Israel) featured Weight Watchers, a hugely overweight woman panted in to sign up before the program finished. A fat schoolteacher took her class to visit a Bedouin camp, and the head of the tribe said approvingly, "Do you know how many cattle you're worth?" The embarrassed teacher lost no time getting to Weight Watchers.

The Jerusalem representative runs her Weight Watcher sessions four times a week. English-language gatherings take place Monday afternoons, and they lean heavily to Americans who have transported themselves and their weight problems five thousand miles. Morning Hebrew-language gatherings are made up principally of housewives, some of whom bring their babies, knitting, or food. During a typical meeting one huge woman nibbled constantly; she began with green peppers and wound up with apples. When she saw other people watching her, she turned to face the wall—and kept eating.

Ephraim Goldman, a thirty-three-year-old bank clerk, proudly showed an old picture in which he looked the double of the late King Farouk in His Majesty's expansive prime. Goldman came to Weight Watchers when a friend said, "What have you got to lose?" It was plain enough: about 130 pounds. He has lost 90 of them, and to show how much better he feels, he races up the stairs of the bank two steps at a time.

One of the star Weight Watchers is Yosef Shumeh, an Israeli in his fifties who came from Iraq in 1951 and has a large fruit and vegetable stand in Jerusalem's central market. He came to Mrs. Amsel in desperation, complaining that his work made it impossible for him to lose weight: "Half my cucumbers I sell, and half I eat."

And he was crazy about *kubeh,* a Middle Eastern specialty made with meat and rice.

"We don't eat *kubeh* at Weight Watchers," said Mrs. Amsel.

"How can I live without *kubeh?*" he asked.

"I looked at that fat man who could hardly breathe," Mrs. Amsel recalled, "and in one week without *kubeh* he lost nine pounds. Three months later a man came from the same community and started insisting on *kubeh.* Yosef said, 'Who needs *kubeh?* You can do without it.'"

Jewish Farmers

THESE ARE THE MEN who sowed the corn that fed the roosters which woke the sons who picked the beets which made the borsht in the house that Jake built.

They are survivors of a headier day when the Catskills swarmed with Jewish farmers who cultivated vegetables, raised dairy cattle, and fed their best lines to garment workers on summer holiday. In this borsht belt, famous for Jewish jokes, the farmers—like the jokes—have seen better days.

"The Jewish farmer is getting to be a rare bird—for that you need a hunter," said Theodore Norman, managing director of the Baron de Hirsch Fund whose mission during about eighty years has been to help Jews settle on the land.

David Wagner has lived on a farm most of his life. "There was a time when I couldn't tell you the names of all the Jewish farmers—it would have taken me hours," he said. "Now I could sit down and write you a list."

His grandfather came from Eastern Europe to New York's Sullivan County in the late twenties and built a struggling model of the Catskill boardinghouse farm. "My grandfather was a cloak-and-suiter who wanted to get out of the unhealthy city," said Mr. Wagner. "But he and my father wound up working in the city to keep the farm alive."

Later, Wagner went to Cornell's agricultural school. "My wife comes from the Bronx," he said. "I told her relatives I was a poultry major at college, and for several months they thought I was a poetry major. I think they would have preferred a poetry major."

Eventually, he took charge of egg production for the Inter-County Farmers Cooperative Association. In each of six chicken houses there are forty thousand hens and one rooster, the rooster for psychological reasons. "My psychology," explained Wagner. "If there's a rooster around, it makes me feel more like a farmer."

"Jews weren't farmers in the countries where they emigrated from. We're doing what our grandparents couldn't do—and in view of the present market, maybe they were right."

Wagner, who is in his forties and looks robust, takes one thing personally. "Talk about psychosomatic diseases!" he said. "I can't say cholester . . . cholest . . . The human being has a mechanism to adjust to cho. . . . I eat four double-yolked eggs a day, and my you-know-what count is below normal. If I live to ninety, the medical profession will have a lot of explaining to do."

• • •

Gussie Rados came to South Fallsburg from a European Displaced Persons camp. "Always in Europe I dreamed of having a home and sitting under a tree and seeing the birds and nature," she said. "We was nature lovers, but we didn't know from a kangaroo.

"When we came here we saw chickens, a building, green grass; and this impressed us. The farmer here took us around the house twenty times, and I was a *greener* and I thought, 'So many rooms!' I thought a chicken lays three, four eggs a day—so much money! So we bought the farm and we bought chickens, and the next day all the chickens were dead. We didn't know what or when. But we said we're going to survive—we had worse times in Europe.

"We reached already to fifteen thousand hens. Now we only have a few thousand hens and we sell the eggs to people who pass by and to grocers, and our living we make from the bungalows. If it's going to be another five years, the Jewish farmer is finished. I'm thinking a lot of time, Was worth it? Was worth it?"

• • •

Morris Heller is one of the rare local farmers who grows vegetables. His father brought the family up to the town of Swan Lake during the Depression and then went back to his job in the garment industry.

"My big mistake was milking my first cow—I was nine or ten—because then I had to go on doing it," Heller said. "A rainy day was wonderful for me, since it meant I didn't have to work."

About twenty of his hundred acres are planted with a full range of vegetables, and he walks the rows proudly, his weathered face beaming. "During the weeding it's more a mental battle than physical work," he said. "I've had kids who came up from New York—all Jewish boys—who want to work on a farm, but they never last more than a day.

"If I could find a way to sell weeds, I'd give up planting

vegetables and grow weeds. One year my daughter Amy and I hand-weeded an acre of corn together. She was very good at it, but I had to encourage her by telling her a lot of stories. And we'd have races. At the end I owed her forty ice cream sodas, ten banana splits and eighteen sundaes."

Years ago Heller began collecting books on natural history and selling them by catalog. Now each winter he works diligently at the book trade and travels twenty thousand miles visiting other dealers and book sales. "One year I got too interested in books and I got behind in my farm work," he said. "What suffered? I suffered. The vegetables are my mainstay, but the bookselling's more interesting, because then I deal with people, and the rest of the time I deal with vegetables."

• • •

When he was twelve years old, Max Dwosh was working as a tinsmith in Poland. He and his wife came to America in 1951 and made a down payment on a rundown farm. "We were starving," she said. "All we had was five dollars a week for food."

"We worked day and night," he said. "Our dream was to build ourselves up to be capable to make a decent living. Then there started to be big competition with large corporations. Years pass by and we're getting a little tired of working the way we used to. We were much younger before. Our children saw the way we worked and struggled, and they don't see a use for it—and I wouldn't like them to do it. It's long hours, seven days a week, and you're asking yourself a question—'Is the money worth it?' "

• • •

Irving Goldstein and his wife Regina were born in Poland and came to this country in 1949. He had spent five years—from age fourteen to nineteen—in a concentration camp, and she had been hidden during the war by a Christian family. "We were never children, never had a childhood," she said.

Now they own a large chicken farm. "There is a little secret," she suggested. "After being in a concentration camp and existing on a crust of bread, you're ready to work, and you demand very little out of life. Now, when we would like to take time out, the business holds us. My husband thinks if he's not going to put the chickens to sleep, they won't go to sleep."

"I don't feel like a farmer," he said. "I feel like a slave."

"Very often I feel guilty because we made our life here—so isolated in the country—because of the children," his wife said. "My daughter used to sit at the window for hours. When she heard a car she would say: 'Maybe they'll stop here!'"

• • •

Ben Gulkow, who was born near Minsk, came to this country in 1948 and started farm work as the partner of an observant Jew. "For him Friday was Friday, and Saturday was Saturday, and Sunday was after Saturday," Gulkow complained. "He was bossing and I was working."

In 1951 he bought his own farm. "I work fifteen days a week—you start at five o'clock in morning and finish at ten o'clock in night," he said. "I ended with three heart attacks in one year and then open-heart surgery. That's from aggravation and hard work.

"How long can you lose money? I have a son, a Cornell graduate in agriculture. After a while he said, 'Pa, you have nothing, I have nothing. How can I stay on farm?'

"All my friends from the bad times in Europe are in Israel now. I still think of going to Israel—that's the only dream I have."

Summer Camp

IN DEFIANCE OF biological law, there seemed to be about six parents for each child. On Parents' Day at Camp Shomria, near Liberty, New York, the soccer field became a picnic area, appetite rampant unto the farthest horizon. Then it became a parade ground, with multitudes marching to the call of the child.

Everywhere blossomed scenes of touching domesticity. "The trouble with you is that you never think of anyone else—only yourself," a grown-up sister chided her brother. From the culprit—silence close to tears. Camper 1 to Camper 2: "Did they bring your yellow raisins?" Camper 2: "Two boxes!"

For thirty years now, under the sponsorship of Hashomer Hatzair, an Israeli kibbutz federation, this camp has been running on socialist lines. No one on the staff is paid, except for two women who work in the kitchen, and most decisions are taken collectively by the counselors, ages sixteen to eighteen. Counselors never accept tips, but who can resist a chocolate *babka* or a Jewish danish?

En route from New York City, the road to camp runs along Liberty's main street, and parents on their pilgrimage make their ritual stop at Katz's bake shop. This is a Catskillian shrine of such classical grandeur, independent spirit and rococo bounty as to make Manhattan bakeries appear Appalachian.

"Isn't it beautiful!" said Tirtzah Ben-Ami, a fourteen-year-old camper, biting into a pecan roll.

Ralph Dublinsky had gotten his children's shopping orders and followed them to the letter. "Liat asked for candies, cakes, and patches for her pants," he said. "Jana wanted delicatessen, comic books and one of my T-shirts."

"Knowing that my daughter would have to share, we brought up more food," said Dan Stallman.

"I brought thirty-eight pieces of chicken for four people," said a friend.

Bunkmates and tentmates pool their spending money and their loot. Trunks are safe deposit boxes—always open—and campers are free to make food and/or money withdrawals when they please. They are expected to exercise socialist discipline. As the days progress and socialist ideals affirm themselves, the period lengthens between day of deposit and day of withdrawal.

Exercising remote supervision are four kibbutzniks from Hashomer Hatzair. The federation has about fifteen hundred American members, many of whom are planning to emigrate to Israel. "Sometimes we have brilliant kids of nineteen or twenty who go out and change the world," said Israel Stashefsky of Kibbutz Sasa, "and sometimes we don't."

One father, dragged along to his daughter's tent, discovered that her cot was so inviting that he stretched out on it, closed his eyes and spent a delightful visiting day.

He missed the last great events, in the open-air theater

improvised on the soccer field. The prevailing theme seemed to be self-mockery. "You are about to witness a program which has taken centuries of tradition and training," noted the announcer. "Entertainment which is not so entertainmenty," said Tirtzah.

There were Israeli dances, and a hefty proportion of the dancers seemed to have spent the previous weeks at Katz's, trying bread-and-butter socialism. "Dancing doesn't seem to be the way to lose weight," said Geno Rice, one of the visitors.

Tirtzah's group sang "Praise for the Sultan," borrowed from an Israeli comic operetta which tells of a greedy sultan who got so fat he could eat no more. "For this," the song concluded, "give praise to God."

Chopped Liver

CHOPPED LIVER is a delicacy on the table, but suddenly it was a glut on the market. Prices sank to a twenty-year low; supplies rose to an all-time high.

Harvey Potkin of Kosher King Meat Products had just come back from Israel, and his report was bleak: "Israel is oversupplied with product. The market fell out of the bottom."

Sidney Schweid, a meat man from Paterson, New Jersey, brought equally fresh gloom. "Losing 10 cents a pound, I offered them calves' livers at 45 cents, and they wouldn't take them. There's a glut of livers."

Abe Lebewohl, the owner of the Second Avenue Delicatessen who traditionally distributed free chopped liver canapés to customers waiting for tables, could hardly credit his good fortune. "You took four ribs," his meat supplier said to him. "Please, Abe, take a few livers."

The National Provisioner Daily Market and News Service, keeper of the records, reported that in twenty-ton stockyard lots, selected heifer and steer liver was 18 cents a pound. Two years earlier it had been up to 61½. Not in twenty years had it been as low as 19.

"Edible fat that goes into cooking grease costs 16 cents—and it doesn't have nutritional value," Mr. Potkin complained. "And here we have a highly nutritious item like liver for 18 cents."

"The nature of people being what they are, even though they like a good bargain, they're not going to eat something that doesn't agree with their taste. I'm the biggest distributor of kosher liver in the country. My kids—a thirteen, a ten and a five—you put a piece of liver on the table, they run out of the house."

"I've had a very difficult summer," he said. "Take Weinberger, of Mrs. Weinberg's Kosher Chopped Liver. He is to the liver business what Hebrew National is to franks. Normally he pays me 48 to 55 cents a pound. I can't get him to pay me 30 cents."

"They're falling all over their feet to sell to me," said Sidney Weinberger, president of the company that uses thirty-five hundred pounds of liver daily. "I've been offered prices so low I can't believe them."

While politicians and their professors debated esoteric matters like foreign policy and even morality, liver was going to the dogs—and cats. Cattle were being slaughtered in record numbers, livers accumulated, importers disappeared. Japan, which had jumped into the market a couple of years earlier, had jumped out. The French, guardians of gastronomy, had simply given up dealing with what they called the *crise de foie* (liver crisis).

That left Israel, as usual, struggling with one crisis too many. "I understand Israeli importers have so much liver it's unbelievable," said Alexander Schlesinger of Alex Kosher Meats. "Maybe the place is full," suggested Gus

Goetz of A to Z Kosher Meat Products. "You know, once in a while you get sick of it."

Pinchas Teitz, a rabbi who devotes his artistry to certifying meat as kosher, said Israel was short of foreign currency. "A part of tightening the belt is not buying liver," he suggested.

"Israel is drowning in chopped liver," Rabbi Jacob Savitsky said. "It's a very grave situation. What can they do about it?"

Mrs. Weinberg's Mr. Weinberger, who had answers to perplexing problems at the tip of his tongue, was asked what could be done to save a country drowning in chopped liver. "Other questions I can answer," he said. "That one I can't."

S. J. Perelman

SHAKEN AND SOBERED, a mere shard of his former self, S. J. Perelman has returned from prolonged exposure to the undiscovered country from which no caviller returns. Mutable and trepid, he has shaken the mould of Florida from his plimsolls and is now exorcising the memory.

To hear him tell it, in that quavering voice which passeth understanding, the adventure was *trayf* with dietary peril and plangent with nostalgic heartburn. As his audible hum swelled into plain song, the terrors which drove him to flee the keys of Sarasota became freshly vocal: "A combination of intense boredom and bad cooking."

He went down to Sarasota to share rations and quarters with fellow authors Lillian Hellman, Albert Hackett, and Frances Goodrich, who is Mr. Hackett's wife. "Lilly did the cooking and we did the eating," said Mr. Perelman, lapsing into *recitativo*. "Lilly has a feeling for cooking, but the couple who took over when she left didn't have the same feeling."

"Whenever the dishwasher was being loaded, I fluttered

around the kitchen pretending to be slightly angry because the Hacketts had taken my job—a beautiful bit of acting which would have left John Barrymore at a disadvantage. There were no real disputes, since we were already like tempered Damascus steel—we knew each other's vagaries.

"Most of the time we sat around a pool speculating that this is what the average person believes writers do. When we felt energetic we discussed the gossip that Lilly obtained by telephone from her secretary in New York. I think I saw Lilly go into the pool once. She never, never saw me go into the pool once.

"The only other energy shortage that bothered me was the total lack of energy that assailed me at the typewriter, although Florida is one of the few places I've been where work was more attractive than the place. My fellow Damascans were infuriated with the fact that I seemed to be working and they were not. They thought it was braggadocio on my part, that I was trying to humiliate them. So they set up a Ping-Pong table. Those people would do anything to avoid work."

Without waiting to regain the equable tenor of his ways, he hurried on. "I don't think I met a real Floridian, or heard a single Florida idiom except 'Come back and see us real soon'—that vinegary and acid-sweet mixture they throw at you," he said, tugging at his neatly understated Prince de Galles jacket emblazoned with the family arms—calves rampant, loins couchant. "Everybody is from Michigan or Texas, determined to enjoy the worst of all possible worlds. There are an awful lot of retirement villages and mobile-home villages, which lends no end of character to the general air of eyesore."

Waving aside interruptions, he plunged into the heart of his refrain: "Stores selling broadloom carpets, ladies' shoe stores, motorboat mausoleums, fruiteries that ship oranges north to your dearest relatives. Prices are high, but only for food and other necessities of life, and that doesn't bother anybody except the people.

"We brought the essentials with us from New York and dressed very conservatively, which caused some uplifted eyebrows among those citizens who had the energy to lift them. Our costumes ranged from a towel wrapped around our condominiums to a pair of chinos enclosing our bungalows."

For those less provident, there is a supermarket. "It has something called 'real New York Jewish rye,' which is the product of a mad scientist who has never seen New York or set eyes on a member of this ethnic group," Mr. Perelman said. "The customers walk in a circle around the bread, eyeing it suspiciously. I stood there in a state of suppressed fury, just hoping someone would come along and take a package, and I would pinion his arms and ask him what was his basis of comparison. Hellman said she saw three people in Sarasota who knew of leavened and unleavened and the *kasha* in the rye, but I assured her it was a mirage on an unseen-of scale.

"There is also off-the-street mayhem in the restaurants, where the noise is like the stock exchange at the height of the trading. Since the food is perhaps the worst served anywhere on this continent, I can sympathize with the rabble."

His voice trailing off, Mr. Perelman acknowledged that he was dying to return. "I'm training a team of wild horses to take me back," he said.

Tour

A BLUE STATION wagon crossed Times Square, and as it drove east on 46th Street, the eight Roman Catholic girls inside merrily sang *"Shabbat Shalom!"* (Welcome, Sabbath!) The driver, Rabbi Bernard M. Cohen, beamed, took his right hand from the wheel, and conducted.

"Rabbi," asked a passenger, "what would Tevye, in *Fiddler on the Roof,* have said about a rabbi who went through a red light?"

"A very good question," said the rabbi, blushing. "Now, girls, let's think. What would Tevye say about going through a red light?"

"It's only a machine, and I'm a man," was one suggestion.

"The light keeps changing, and I remain the same," was another.

"Very good," said the rabbi, and when the light was green he turned south on Second Avenue.

It was the sixth day of an eight-day visit by students from St. Mary-of-the-Woods College, outside Terre Haute, to

New York's Jewish community. For the tour, plus nine lectures by the rabbi, the students will get one or two credits toward graduation. Each of the girls contributed $175 for expenses, and $40 to $80 tuition for the inter-session course "Searching and Discovering the Jewish Community of New York."

Rabbi Cohen, a Reform clergyman who was born in New York, said he was the first rabbi on the faculty of any Roman Catholic college. He divided his time between the campus and his congregation, and liked to think that in Terre Haute—which was once a Ku Klux Klan stronghold—ecumenism finally flourished.

The women in his charge (his wife and a woman friend came along as chaperones) had already attended Hasidic prayers in the Williamsburg section of Brooklyn, toured WEVD ("the station that speaks your language"), and sampled specialties at Katz's Delicatessen, Streit's Matzo Factory, and Shapiro's Kosher Wine Company. They had heard lectures on Talmud and the generation gap, and on the survival of Yiddish. Rabbi Cohen enjoined his students to understand Judaism "not as a piece of *gefilte* fish or a sour pickle, not as something gastrointestinal, but as something cerebral."

"You're missionaries this week," he said jokingly as the car passed 27th Street.

"Rabbi," said a voice in the back, "could you put the window down a little bit?"

"What does this have to do with the missionaries?" he asked.

"You'll have frozen missionaries unless you put the window down," the young woman answered.

At Kaplan's Pickle Stand, the rabbi invited his students to take pickles out of a barrel. "But make it fast," said Mr. Kaplan. "It's Friday. I have to do business."

As the class paused for one of many quick sidewalk homilies, a woman strolled up. Hearing the rabbi talk about "a yarmulke, a skullcap, a cardinal's cap," she blurted: "A religious hypocrite! Worse than an atheist! Don't be a hypocrite!"

A second woman asked what was going on. When she heard the group was studying Judaism on the Lower East Side, she announced, "There isn't a trace of Judaism here anymore. Ask me and I'll tell you."

At a sour tomato stand, the class noted a sign saying "Closed for Vacation—Thank God," and then everyone went into Yonah Schimmel's *knish* bakery. The owner, Arthur Berger, explained that his grandfather had started baking *knishes* in 1910, after proving unsuccessful as a teacher.

"He was a successful teacher," corrected the rabbi. "He just didn't make a living from it."

To walk off the pickles, *knishes* and cheese blintzes (since it was Good Friday, no one ate meat), the group set off on foot for *The Forward*, where the managing editor welcomed the pilgrims.

"Do you have syndicated columns?" asked Kathy Kelly.

"Our columns are not syndicated," he replied, "because there are two Jewish papers here in New York, and if we syndicated, we'd both be printing the same things. We're probably the only real world newspaper, except for one other one in New York. But that one goes to ambassadors and cabinet ministers. We go to people."

"When we get back to the hotel," Miss Kelly asked the rabbi, "can we go to St. Malachy's Church? They're going to have the Veneration of the Cross."

"Of course, my little Talmud scholar," the rabbi replied.

Haggadah

Of all Jewish classics save perhaps the Bible, the Haggadah—the book of the Seder, the ritual Passover meal—has been the most often reprinted, in over thirty-five hundred editions. Harvard's Professor Yosef H. Yerushalmi, author of the bountifully illustrated and authoritative *Haggadah and History*, called the Haggadah "the book of remembrance and redemption." Participants in the Passover meal think of themselves as being delivered from Egypt and look forward also to future redemption. "Every oppressor is Pharaoh," suggested Professor Yerushalmi "and Egypt every exile."

The Passover meal is a liturgy celebrated not in the synagogue but in the family, and Professor Yerushalmi called it "that orchestration of symbol, ritual and recital for which the Haggadah provides the score." Haggadah means "the telling," as prescribed by Exodus: "And thou shalt tell thy son in that day, saying: It is done because of that which the Lord did for me when I came forth out of Egypt."

To honor the Haggadah, three New York institutions—the Metropolitan Museum of Art, the Jewish Museum, and the Yeshiva University Museum—each in a single Passover season, put on exhibitions of Haggadah treasures.

Professor Harry Bober of New York University's Institute of Fine Arts was guest curator of the Metropolitan's "Passover Story." He is an expert on medieval illuminated manuscripts, but not on Jewish liturgy. "Here I can revel in my incomprehension, bumbling around," he noted.

"I'll show you what I use at the Seder," he said, pulling out a worn sheaf of text untouched by gilt. "This is a Manischewitz Haggadah—they give them away as ads—and the date is whatever-they-put-on-it. If this were a university exhibition I think we'd show the Manischewitz Haggadah as well as the others. But this is the Metropolitan."

At Yeshiva were delights such as a 1695 Amsterdam printed Haggadah which set the enduring style for illustrations down to twentieth-century Jersey City Manischewitz. Here, too, was a 1568 Haggadah from Mantua, Italy, with the familiar illustration of the Messiah on a donkey. Seder participants read the Haggadah as they feast, and this Messiah, en route to eternity, is saddled with the stains of wine. Over the centuries, such erosion by food and wine has been a God-given boon to publishers, assuring a market for new Haggadot.

The Mantua Haggadah was from the collection of the family of Dr. Alfred Moldovan, a New York internist. He used to collect ritual *objets d'art.* "Then the market got flooded with fakes," he said. "I got very nervous, so I turned to books. I figured they're not faking books yet."

At his family Seder, Dr. Moldovan uses a modern Haggadah and adds Orthodox elements from his youth; for example, what he called "the lovely ritual of the plagues."

Traditional Haggadot illustrate the ten plagues visited on Egypt: blood, frogs, lice, wild beasts, blight, boils, hail, locusts, darkness and slaying of the firstborn.

Routinely, Haggadot also depict the Passover story's four sons—wise, wicked, simple, and the one who knows not what to ask. Usually the wicked son is portrayed as a soldier. In the Yeshiva reserves, the wondrous illuminations of Polish-born Arthur Szyk (1894–1951) depict the wicked son as a fat cigar-smoking Polish-Jewish merchant. More alluring as modern Israeli pioneers are the figures modeled on Szyk's wife and daughter.

The Jewish Museum had its 1695 Amsterdam Haggadah open to show the wicked soldier. Also on display were eleven paintings by Ben Shahn for his edition of the Haggadah.

In text, illustrations and songs, Haggadot combine—according to the traditions, beliefs, whims and imaginations of their authors, editors, artists and composers—texts and models ancient and modern, Biblical and rabbinical, somber and diverting, authentic and anachronistic. A 1526 Prague Haggadah shows Egyptian cities with the architecture of Prague, and a husband pointing bitter herbs at his wife, "for it is said that a bad wife is more bitter than death" (Ecclesiastes 7:26). These iconographic traditions fell victim to time and liberating passions, but other stereotypes survived: Pharaoh is often still shown in a tub.

The great Prague Haggadah also has a woodcut of hounds chasing hares—a mnemonic device suggested the sequence for a Saturday night Seder: an acronym of the initial Hebrew letters YaKeNHaZ, sounding like the German for hare-hunt. In a later Haggadah, the hares escape, whence the allegoric interpretation: hares (Jews) escape dogs (oppressors).

When Haggadot turn up in Italian editions, borders sprout

out chubby cherubs carousing; the simple son emerges as the Italian buffoon. In Italian editions, Abraham is being transported across the river into Canaan not in a rowboat but in a gondola. Italy's artists found a ready image for the wise son or wise father: they lifted Michelangelo's image of Jeremiah from the Sistine Chapel.

A Basle Haggadah features one illustration copied from a depiction of the Last Supper—that Supper may have been a Seder, with matzoh seen as Christ's body, wine his blood. Cologne's 1838 Haggadah has music by Isaac Offenbach, father of the Jacques who composed such secular triumphs as *La Vie Parisienne* and *Tales of Hoffmann*.

One of the least likely editions of the Haggadot reproduced in Professor Yerushalmi's volume was in the London *Times* in 1840, to refute the Damascus blood libel which led to the torture of Jews there.

With the entry of Jews into art's mainstream, this century, came a renaissance in Haggadah art, with editions illustrated by celebrated artists such as Reuven Rubin and Leonard Baskin. A "Polychrome Historical Haggadah for Passover," by Rabbi Jacob Freedman, features color-coded signposts to indicate sources of the Haggadah.

At least 437 commentaries by rabbis and scholars have been incorporated into Haggadot, and books have been devoted to the meaning of a single Seder song. Professor Yerushalmi suggests that commentaries tell much, not only about the text they illuminate, but about "the changing religious and ideological concerns of Jews through the centuries."

Haggadot are a guide to the linguistic complexity imposed by persecution and exile. While Haggadot normally have Hebrew text and translation into a vernacular—in Israel the vernacular is the Hebrew—a Renaissance Haggadah for crypto-convert Marranos was printed in Amsterdam entirely in Spanish, for the Marranos knew no Hebrew. Another Marrano Haggadah was printed after the discovery, early this century, that the Portuguese Marranos, forcibly converted in 1497, had not disappeared, or as Professor Yerushalmi put it, "They had only disappeared from view."

One Haggadah printed in Bulgaria was in Ladino (Judeo-Spanish normally written in Hebrew characters) in Cyrillic characters; in Istanbul a Ladino text was written in the Latin alphabet according to the rules of modern Turkish.

In the English-praying world, text innovations are common, with borrowing from sources as disparate as Anne Frank and Albert Einstein. Leftist Jews have produced radical Haggadot. There are over a thousand kibbutz editions of Haggadot, with questions often shifting from ritual curiosity ("Why is this night different from all other nights?") to fresh longing: "And why do men fight instead of giving a helping hand to one another...?"

The literature is rich with parodies. One parody deplores the poverty of Hebrew authors, another the suffering of yeshiva students; and a third compares the life of East European Jewish teachers to slaves in Egypt: "How does teaching differ from all other professions in the world? All other professions enrich, and their practitioners eat and drink and are happy all the days of the year. But teachers groan and despair even on this night."

One Haggadah satirizes capitalism, another attacks the czarist meat tax, and a third ridicules the czar himself. In New York's 1904 election campaign, "The Ten Plagues of Tammany" vituperated against corruption.

Many Haggadot now include a Ritual of Remembrance for the six million Jews killed by the Nazis, with verses by Yitzhak Katzenelson, who was killed in Auschwitz: "I weep in anguish by day and by night./Why, my Lord; wherefore, O God?"

The Soviet Union has produced at least two antireligious versions, one of which, "Against the Mildew of the Ages," suggests: "May annihilation overcome all the outdated rabbinic laws and customs, yeshivas and Jewish elementary schools, which blacken and enslave the people." Israel has published a bilingual Haggadah—Hebrew and Russian—for Soviet immigrants, to mark the new exodus.

Green Park

GREEN PARK, on East Overcliff Drive in Bournemouth, England, was not out of *Jane Eyre* or *Wuthering Heights*. In fact it was rarely out of anything. This was the site of the ever abnormal granary, the perenially bubbling soda bottle, the eternally enticing *kishka*.

If Grossinger's was a vast jangling glory in the American Catskills, Green Park was a gentle glow on the British seafront. There was hardly an Anglo-Jewish family of note which had not favored the hotel with its custom and appetites. "We cater for the very much better type of individual," Reuben Marriott, owner and manager since 1943, used to say. "If certain classes of people came here we wouldn't feel comfortable, and I don't think they would either. We cater for the better end of the business."

Mr. Marriott, a hotelier of great repute in Britain, was not related to the American hotelier of the same surname, and the English accent did make a difference. So did the kosher cuisine. In America, Jewish jokes were often situated in Grossinger's or in the Concord, or at worst in the Fontainebleau, but in Britain they were honored by being unfailingly fixed in Green Park.

A hotel guest in the typical English hotel might count himself fortunate—or unfortunate—to be allowed to be lonely. At Green Park one was lonely only by choice, for strangers were quickly drawn into whatever conversations were proceeding in the lounge. Mr. Marriott recalled one guest, who'd gone into another Jewish hotel in Bournemouth, returning to exult, "I didn't know a single person."

To explain why they were staying at another hotel, people apologized that they couldn't get into Green Park. For Passover it was almost impossible to win admission without sterling recommendations. "At Pesach we'd say no to everybody—and then we'd sort out the people we'd like to have," explained Mr. Marriott. He telephoned the fortunate chosen people and asked them—with the air of a prince offering a baronetcy—if they'd be coming for Passover. Prices went up then, and many would-be clients—despite tearful pleas to be allowed to spend the baronet's ransom—could not even get waiting-list rights. "Very expensive for Pesach because you ate round the clock," explained one guest, in tones clipped and peremptory.

One favored couple had not missed a single Pesach or year-end holiday in thirty years, and came for other holidays as well. They were admired for fidelity and envied for grace and favor.

Mr. Marriott himself was the most spoiled man in the British Empire. His wife Sarah and her three unmarried sisters helped him run the hotel and fussed over him constantly. The five lived in an apartment across from the hotel. Sarah Marriott (née Richman) was the social arbiter at Green Park, astonishingly knowledgeable on the glosses of class distinction. Her role was compared to the Queen Mother's—all fun and no responsibilities. Judy Richman did the hotel accounts, Ray Richman handled reservations and reception, and Hannah Richman was in charge of catering—kitchen, dining room and room service. "Mr. Marriott manages us all," said Judy Richman.

There were two other married sisters not associated with the hotel. One was on the staff until her marriage, and the other married before the Marriott reign. There were also three brothers, and one served as cantor for holiday services. The Chief Rabbi was a regular guest for the Simchat Torah holiday.

What was once the hotel ballroom became the synagogue, with the most comfortable pews in any place of worship anywhere—the period was authentic Louis Kahn's.

The four sisters managed by Mr. Marriott collaborated to do the *gros point* for the fifty green easy chairs in the hotel's formal drawing room, from which children under twelve were barred. Sarah Marriott did the most difficult portions while waiting to play her hand in the nightly card games.

Kalooki—thirteen-card rummy, best played by five people—was the local game, and stakes in the card room were usually moderate. Sarah Marriott was lady of the card chamber—it was she who introduced one guest player to another. Noted Toby Black of London, a frequent guest, "If Sarah said 'Meet Mr. X, a very strong player,' it meant you got a good table and a strong light on it. 'Nice player' meant not a good player, don't make her your partner, and the lights will be poor."

A strong player such as Mrs. Black would be allowed to sit near the switches for air conditioning in the summer and heating in the winter. "When you reached the top table you were at the pinnacle," said Louis Plotnikoff, a regular client from Scotland. "Nobody got there without deserving the honor."

In the card room the top table was literally top—on a raised dais where a band used to sit.

Many nonobservant clients skipped Friday night services and had a flutter at the local casino. When they returned by taxi, the driver usually asked, "Do you want the Shabbas entrance, or the normal one?" "Shabbas entrance" was a euphemism for being left on the street corner instead of being deposited at the hotel door—where the appearance of a Jewish client motorized on the Sabbath could offend the Orthodox.

Scrabble was a permitted diversion on the Sabbath. But since writing was not permitted, each player kept a book on his lap—open to the page whose number was the same as his score.

Saturdays there was a promenade along the cliff top until noon. Sporting gentlemen then retired to their rooms to keep in touch with the horse races, and the telephone lines hummed. "If you were staying at Green Park, you could have as much credit as you wanted with the bookmaker," said Mr. Plotnikoff.

"Most people here had Shabbas jackets," he noted. "They kept wearing them out putting their hand in to get cigarettes—and then remembering it's Shabbas."

On Saturday nights a group of kalooki fervents waited anxiously for Mr. Marriott's signal that the Sabbath was over. Leslie Keisner, a regular visitor, called this ultimate game of patience "the time when the minutes were the longest in the week."

Mr. Marriott enforced a TV blackout in the lounge on Sabbath, but the year England reached the finals of the soccer World Cup, guests rebelled. Mr. Marriott finally caved in and allowed the TV to be turned on—provided the curtains were drawn. His wife cheered with gusto when the British did well. "*Lig in dr'erd!*" (Lie low!), she shouted in her understated Yiddish when a German player went down.

Before Green Park had a license to sell liquor, it held twice weekly cocktail parties—free—for its guests. Eventually there was a wine waiter, who got many more calls for soft drinks than for alcohol. Typical order: "We'll have a shandy (beer and ginger ale), a gin and tonic, and two cups of tea."

"We made a cheesecake that was unique even by American standards, a marron *gâteau* that was marvelous, a strawberry Romanoff, a *cassata*. And I tasted everything. Our staff was German-Italian-Polish-English-Spanish-Scottish-Austrian-Swiss and one something-that-I-don't-know, perhaps Persian."

For two years Hannah Richman had two teachers giving the staff daily English lessons. Then she decided to simplify matters and began taking lessons herself. She learned Italian and picked up a good deal of Spanish.

The life of the dining room staff was the restaurant manager, Mimmo Zacchia. When he was twenty-one years old he was at the Venice Lido Excelsior Hotel and served the Marriotts there. They were so impressed that they lured him away. The Excelsior forgave them, and then began sending Green Park more young waiters who wanted to learn English.

"I come from a very religious Catholic family, and for a while I didn't know if I was coming or going," said Mr. Zacchia. "I tasted *gefilte* fish once, and it's not really an Italian dish."

On Friday nights he circulated discreetly through the dining room, offering paper yarmulkes to men improvident enough to have turned up without head covering.

The main course at the *table d'hôte* lunch was a choice of three fish (or all three, if the guest desired). Said Mr. Zacchia: "We always had three other fish as well, and guests could order any dishes they pleased. What we put on the menu was just a suggestion."

Meat dishes were served at dinner, except on Saturdays, when the meat came at lunch. Except on the Sabbath, a four-piece Italian orchestra played nostalgic Italian favorites, plus a lively seasoning of Yiddish and Hebrew melodies.

Morning tea was served in bed. Afternoon and evening teas, with unlimited helpings of cake, were served with alacrity—as though there were not a moment to lose in the unceasing struggle with hunger. For late cardplayers, cheese and biscuits and more tea were on tap. Hot chocolate was always available for those who had trouble falling asleep after kalooki.

There was never any charge for extras in food, coffee, tea and the like. "They were on a good wicket," said Mascha Sanson, a regular guest, "because nobody had any strength to eat between meals." Porters were nonetheless forever going round the halls with trays of food, trying to tempt defenseless and unwary clients.

The ideal Green Park guest was described as one who was the same height both ways. One regular client complained to Sarah Marriott when the all-in price per day was raised from 10 guineas to 11 (then about $29). "You're killing me," she said. "It was hard enough to eat everything when the price was 10 guineas."

The Marriotts and the Richmans had an extraordinary

memory for social detail and personal idiosyncrasy. They never forgot a name, a marriage, a divorce, or a preference for a particular delicacy. For one guest it was a glass filled with celery stalks, for another a special sugar substitute, for a third Melba toast. At breakfast there was a selection of about thirty-five different jams and marmalades.

Green Park had sixty rooms, of which fifty-seven were doubles, and a staff of ninety-five. Said Mr. Marriott: "Normally we were overstaffed so in the event of the unforeseen happening it shouldn't be noticed by the guests."

The housekeeper knew what each guest wanted. She therefore complained to one of the Marriotts: "Why didn't you tell me it's the wrong Mr. Goldstein? I have all the square pillows out for him."

"I had an Italian chef who made the most wonderful stuffed neck you ever tasted, and marvelous *gefilte* fish," said Hannah Richman. "A veal *marengo* is supposed to have crayfish—which isn't kosher—so we substituted a kosher garnish. We make *coq au vin* with kosher claret.

"Our Austrian-Swiss pastry chef was incredible—he made all our *pâtisserie*, dinner rolls, *challah* for Sabbath, sweets, *petits fours*, afternoon biscuits for tea, everything except the bread for toast. And on Pesach he took apart his ovens to make sure they were in order for the holiday.

Exhilaration from overeating was not an unknown ailment. One new client left the dining room after her first Green Park breakfast exclaiming with delighted astonishment: "It's been years since I had indigestion after breakfast!"

Fortunately, this was a country where general practitioners still made house calls. Daily between 11 A.M. and 1 P.M. the local doctor appeared automatically—in rain or in shine, in sickness or in health. Nobody had to call him. As a longtime guest explained with a smile: "If you felt all right you wrote down, '*Don't* call at room 22.'"

Routine at Green Park was eventually enshrined as tradition. "Smoked salmon was featured for Saturday dinner, borsht was a Sunday night special," noted Toby Black.

She recalled running into Ronnie Cohen, who had been at the hotel four weeks, and asking how much longer he was staying. "Two more smoked salmons and a borsht," Cohen replied.